CATEGORY PIRATES

A Marketer's Guide To Category Design

How To Escape The "Better" Trap, Dam The Demand, And Launch A Lightning Strike Strategy

First published by Category Pirates 2021

Copyright © 2021 by Category Pirates

All rights reserved. No part of this publication may be reproduced, stored or transmitted in any form or by any means, electronic, mechanical, photocopying, recording, scanning, or otherwise without written permission from the publisher. It is illegal to copy this book, post it to a website, or distribute it by any other means without permission.

Category Pirates asserts the moral right to be identified as the author of this work.

Category Pirates has no responsibility for the persistence or accuracy of URLs for external or third-party Internet Websites referred to in this publication and does not guarantee that any content on such Websites is, or will remain, accurate or appropriate.

Designations used by companies to distinguish their products are often claimed as trademarks. All brand names and product names used in this book and on its cover are trade names, service marks, trademarks and registered trademarks of their respective owners. The publishers and the book are not associated with any product or vendor mentioned in this book. None of the companies referenced within the book have endorsed the book.

First edition

ISBN: 978-1-956934-13-7

Editing by Nicolas Cole
Narration by Christopher Lochhead
Narration by Eddie Yoon

This book was professionally typeset on Reedsy.
Find out more at reedsy.com

Contents

Meet The Pirates	iv
What Other Pirates Have To Say	ix
Acknowledgements	xi
1 A New Category Of Human	1
2 The Big Brand Lie	23
3 The "Better" Trap	47
4 How To Dam The Demand	63
5 The Lightning Strike Strategy	79
6 Rethinking Black Friday & Discount Marketing	122
7 How To Create Content That Matters	141
Subscribe To Category Pirates	174

Meet The Pirates

What is Category Pirates?

Category Pirates is the authority on Category Creation and Category Design.

Every Wednesday (ish), we publish a "mini-book" for the radically different—who want to see, design, and dominate categories of consequence.

Topics include:

- How to create new categories and redesign old ones.
- The Magic Triangle, The 9 Levers, The Category Design Scorecard, and dozens of frameworks for how to create and design new categories in the world.
- Case studies for how successful companies have successful created and/or redesigned existing categories (and where other companies have gone wrong).
- Motivational examples of the power of creating and investing in category creators such as Tesla, Netflix, Amazon, Airbnb, and more.

Every new edition of the newsletter goes directly to your inbox.

- Free subscribers receive snippets of our "mini-books."
- Paying subscribers receive our full "mini-books" every week.

"Why join the Navy if you can be a pirate?" - Steve Jobs

You can hop aboard the pirate ship and subscribe here: categorypirates.substack.com

Meet The Pirates: Eddie Yoon

Eddie Yoon has written more on category strategy for Harvard Business Review than any other person.

Eddie is the founder of EddieWouldGrow, LLC, a think tank and advisory firm on growth strategy, and Co-Creator of Category Pirates.

Previously, he was one of the senior partners at The Cambridge Group, a strategy consulting firm. His work over the past two decades has driven over **$8 billion dollars of annual incremental revenue.** In particular, 8 of his clients have doubled or tripled in revenue in less than 8 years. Eddie is one of the world's leading experts on finding and monetizing Superconsumers to grow and create new categories.

He is the author of the book ***Superconsumers:*** *A Simple, Speedy and Sustainable Path to Superior Growth* (Harvard Business School Press, 2016). His book was named as one of the Best Business Books of 2017 by Strategy & Business. Eddie is also the author of over 100 articles, including "Make Your Best Customers Even Better" (Harvard Business Review magazine, March 2014) and "Why It Pays to Be a Category

Creator" (Harvard Business Review magazine, March 2013). Additionally, he has appeared on CNBC and MSNBC, and been quoted in *The Wall Street Journal, The Economist,* and *Forbes* for his predictions on future category potential of publicly traded companies, as well as been a keynote speaker at industry-leading events in the U.S., Canada, Kenya, Australia, New Zealand, Denmark, the UK and Japan.

Eddie holds an AB in Political Science and Economics from the University of Chicago. Born and raised in Hawaii, he went to the Punahou School in Honolulu. Today, Eddie lives in Chicago with his wife and three children.

Meet The Pirates: Nicolas Cole

Nicolas Cole is one of the most prolific digital writers in the world.

"Cole" as he's known, is an author, viral writer, ghostwriter, and serial "writing entrepreneur." He is the Co-founder of Ship 30 for 30 (a cohort-based community to help people start writing online), Digital Press (a ghostwriting agency for founders, executives, and industry leaders), and Category Pirates. He's been writing online since he was 17 years old—and to date has accumulated hundreds of millions of views on his work.

In 2015, Cole became the #1 most-read writer on Quora (a Question/Answer website with more than 300 million users). And in 2016, he was one of *Inc Magazine's* Top 10 contributing writers, bringing in millions of page views for the publication. His work has been republished all across the Internet, including: *TIME, Forbes, Fortune, Business Insider,*

CNBC, Harvard Business Review, and more.

Over the years, Cole has written more than 3,000 articles online, as well as thousands more under other people's names. He has ghostwritten for hundreds of Silicon Valley founders, Fortune 500 executives, renowned venture capitalists and angel investors, Grammy-winning musicians, Olympic athletes, *New York Times* best-selling authors, and more.

Finally, Cole is the author of the best-selling book, *The Art & Business of Online Writing*, which has become a must-read in the digital publishing world.

He lives in Los Angeles but will forever be from Chicago.

Meet The Pirates: Christopher Lochhead

Christopher Lochhead is a multi-time #1 best-selling Amazon author, #1 Apple podcaster, Top 1% business newsletter creator, and is best known as a "godfather" of Category Design.

He is on a mission to help people design a different future. And ALL of his work is co-created with legendary friends and partners—who he is beyond grateful for.

Christopher's two books, *Play Bigger* and *Niche Down*, were the first texts written on the management discipline of Category Design. And the Category Pirates newsletter is the #1 paid newsletter on the subject, with the Category Pirates "mini-books" consecutively charting at #1 on Amazon. Christopher is also the host of Follow Your Different, a #1 charting business dialogue podcast, and Lochhead on Marketing, a #1 charting Marketing and Category Design podcast.

Christopher is a dyslexic paperboy from Montreal who got thrown out of school at 18 years old. With few other options, he became an entrepreneur, then three-time Silicon Valley public company CMO (Mercury Interactive, Scient, Vantive), and an investor & advisor to over 50 venture-backed startups.

The Marketing Journal calls him "one of the best minds in marketing," NBA legend Bill Walton calls him a "quasar," The Economist calls him "off-putting to some," and some podcast reviewers think he is "overrated" and "not worth it." Podcaster Neil Pearlberg calls Follow Your Different "the worst business podcast," and Podcast Magazine calls Follow Your Different "the best business podcast."

Christopher believes if you're lucky enough to make it to the top of a mountain, you should throw down a rope. So that's what he's trying to do.

You can hop aboard the pirate ship and subscribe here: categorypirates.substack.com

What Other Pirates Have To Say

"If you want to know how to change the world, read Category Pirates. You don't win championships by just being normal."
—**Bill Walton, NBA Hall of Fame Legend**

"Every Category Pirates edition is of immense value. Seriously, it's like a $100,000 MBA with every read."
—**Steve Olsher, Founder of Podcast Magazine**

"When Category Pirates pops up in my inbox, I don't click it right away. I schedule deliberate time, make coffee, and sit in a comfortable chair to read the entire thing. Simply put, this is the most compelling business/marketing letter out."
—**Drew Reggie, Founder of Fly Me To The Fun**

"The value Category Pirates provides is amazing! I am blown away by the quality of their content and how much I learn each week. Reading their newsletter is better than any marketing class in college."
—**Mike Flynn, Founder of Engenius Learning**

"Category Pirates has fundamentally changed how I perceive business. It's unique frameworks have shifted my approach, helped me Name & Claim an emerging category of my own ('cofounder therapy'), and even refined my investment strategy as well (investing

through a category lens). All in all, Category Pirates has accelerated my understanding of business 10x."
    —Dr. Matthew Jones, Founder of Cofounder Clarity

"Category Pirates is a fantastic source of new ideas, thinking and data on Category Creation for me. But it's also one of the best ways to align my executive team. I regularly forward letters to my team, to make sure we are charting the right path to creating this amazing Beauty Health category."
    —Clint Carnell, CEO of the Beauty Health Company

"I love these outstanding mini-books from Category Pirates. I can't wait every week to read them. I have used the Point of View and examples on category creation with so many people in Colgate!"
    —Mukul Deoras, President of Asia and prior CMO of Colgate-Palmolive

Acknowledgements

Written by Pirate Eddie:

I want to thank my Co-Pirate Christopher for his righteous anger.

The original embryo of Category Pirates was born when I received an angry, expletive-riddled call from Christopher when I was in a Costco parking lot on the Big Island of Hawaii in early July of 2019. He was angry *as can be* about someone writing a book about Category Design/Creation. But the real reason why he was angry wasn't that someone else was writing about a topic we both loved and had invested a ton of our careers into. It wasn't that someone had ripped off our writing, research, and work. He was angry that someone was explaining Category Design/Creation so poorly, with a ton of misconceptions that might ultimately mislead many executives, entrepreneurs, and investors into a world of busted IPOs, failed startups, and wasted opportunity.

We firmly believed that Category Creation was the ultimate growth strategy. And we just couldn't stand by and let the aggression stand. It was right then and there in that Costco parking lot that we agreed to write the definitive book on Category Creation/Design, to ensure that the business world going forward would be one full of abundance and creation.

I want to thank my Co-Pirate Cole for his unusual blend of energy and wisdom.

When I was first starting out in my career, I had way more energy than I had wisdom. Hopefully now I have gained more wisdom to offset whatever energy I've lost. For reasons I can't quite figure out, Cole has both double portions of energy and wisdom at the same time.

I met Cole after Christopher reached out to him to help us write the book together. After collaborating on the book for a few months, it became clear that Cole wasn't just helping us synthesize our content and write with one voice, he was contributing as much content as Christopher and I were.

Cole's wisdom is his ability to learn and become great at a myriad of new topics. I'm unsure if it was the time Cole spent becoming a competitive gamer, competitive bodybuilder, a successful entrepreneur, or one of the most viewed writers on Quora. But Cole got up to speed on Category Design/Creation as quickly as Keanu Reeves 'learned Kung Fu' in the Matrix. It was Cole who suggested we "publish" our book chapters one at a time on Substack. It was Cole who suggested we convert our "mini-books" into e-books and audio books on Amazon. It was Cole who designed our Category Pirates business model that is likely to flip the content business on its head.

I am a child of Korean immigrants, born and raised in Hawaii, who spent two decades in the strait-laced profession of management consulting serving the Fortune 500, who is also a follower of Jesus. The three of us make for an odd trio at face-value. But I've never felt more professionally fulfilled, creative and on mission spiritually as God calls me to as I do with Christopher and Cole. Thank you both for being different and letting me be my different.

I love you both dearly.

I want to thank my family for their support of Category Pirates.

Thank you, Miya, for not rolling your eyes too much at the memes we include in our "mini-books." Thank you, Audrey, for letting me be a mentor for your Business Incubator class, where I share many of our Category Pirates lessons. Thank you, Luke, for being nonchalant about all the swearing and manic conversations you overhear when walking by my office on Friday mornings. Thank you to my wife Kristen, for giving me the original freedom, blessing, and encouragement to let me leave my job as a Senior Partner and set up EddieWouldGrow, which in turn gave me the flexibility to embrace being a Category Pirate.

I love you all very much.

1

A New Category Of Human

Dear Category Pirate,

Do you know why the most well-known and successful brands in the world falter?

Do you know the precise moment a Category King or Queen loses control over their kingdom?

When a new category arises (seemingly out of nowhere), the incumbent doesn't topple over because they were unaware of the new Category Queen's existence.

They fall because they dismissed what was happening right before their very eyes.

It's not ignorance.

It's arrogance coupled with the gravitational pull of "the way it is." Because the people profiting in the present want things to stay the same.

"Eh, Keurig and K-Cups are a fad. That will be a small niche."

"Cloud computing is nuts. Major enterprises will never give up their data centers."

"Meh, ride-sharing is a techie thing. Yellow cabs aren't going anywhere."

Until the niche category becomes the dominant category—and what was once new becomes old.

This is called Category Neglect.

Category Neglect doesn't come from people being stupid or lacking sufficient data and resources to spot the headwinds and tailwinds of the future.

It comes from a refusal to acknowledge which direction the wind is really blowing.

Craft beer, *Greek* yogurt, *Cloud* computing and *single-serve* coffee were all trends that could have been spotted and addressed 5-7 years before they crossed over into the mainstream by Anheuser-Busch, General Mills/Yoplait, IBM, and Nestle/Nescafe. These companies collectively spend 9 figures on data to better understand consumer behavior. In its heyday, Anheuser Busch alone spent over a billion dollars on sales and marketing. And back when P&G owned Folgers, an up-and-coming executive went to his boss and told him about an interesting new coffee company out in Seattle called Starbucks. He suggested they look at acquiring them, but was told, "Son, we're not in the food service business. We build the most powerful consumer brands. We are the best marketers in the world. We've got nothing to worry about."

When this happens, incumbents (and their employees and investors) stand to lose billions in market capitalization.

All because they chose contempt over curiosity—*the way it is, over the way it could be.*

The Cautionary Tale of Tymshare

Pirate Christopher remembers a story he was told about a time-sharing company (selling computer time and software packages for users) called Tymshare.

They were having an executive team strategy meeting.

The company was based in Cupertino, California, and a debate ensued about the newly emerging "personal computing" category. And like most incumbents, drunk on the company's current-day profits, the executives in the room dismissed it. They unanimously agreed "personal computing" was nothing to worry about. Simultaneously, through the windows of this exact meeting room where the discussion was happening, you could see the cranes across the street building Apple's new headquarters.

Tymshare's leadership could not see the future being built. Even though it was happening right in front of them. (You can't make this stuff up.)

Netflix Co-founders Marc Randolph and Reed Hastings famously experienced a similar moment when meeting with Blockbuster CEO, John Antioco, in the summer of September, 2000. Randolph and Hastings went into the meeting with a proposition for the two companies to join forces, and ended with a proposition for Blockbuster to acquire Netflix for $50 million.

To which Antioco, "struggling not to laugh," said, "The dot-com hysteria is completely overblown."

He didn't just dismiss Netflix's point of view of the world.

He was borderline insulted by it.

Of course, everyone knows how the Blockbuster vs Netflix situation ended. In 2004, Blockbuster had 9,000 stores globally earning $5.9 billion in revenue. And by 2005, the company had lost 75% of its market value. And in 2010, Blockbuster filed for bankruptcy.

Game over.

Category Neglect happens because the gravitational pull is too strong.

A company gets used to earning hundreds of millions or billions of dollars per year, and thinks it can do no wrong.

The gravitational pull of building a great business takes over and prevents these well-intentioned executives and entrepreneurs from objectively observing the future taking place and capitalizing as a result. They forget what originally made them successful was their ability to change the way "it" was to the way it is—and that, if they aren't careful, someone else can come along and change the way "it" is now *to a new and different way.*

The company becomes deeply invested in the present. And anything that threatens the way it is now is dismissed.

The problem with contempt in business is that it's emotional. It's not objective. When you have contempt, the data can scream in your face that a niche category is growing fast—and you won't be able to hear it. You've enrolled yourself in the "best brand will always win" cult (or worse, the "best product will always win cult) and become myopic.

But contempt is also multi-dimensional, and manifests in ways beyond just contempt for competitors. It's often contempt for customers (like when companies cut costs by lowering quality assuming their customers are too dumb to notice) or jam them into punitive contracts to trap them into buying. It's contempt for their suppliers, forcing ever worsening payment terms on vendors. It is a sad statement when companies invest more in their procurement departments than in their product and category innovation.

Your actions say, "I know better than you," until all of a sudden, you don't.

And you're done.

Contempt weighs you down, and makes it difficult to steer your ship when your life depends on it. The gravity of today's category revenue can pull your eyelids shut to the possibility of a different future.

Native Analogs vs Native Digitals

Typically the last company to adopt a new category paradigm is the number one company in the old category.

Whenever a Category King or Queen begins to neglect their category (aka: dismisses the niche category growing quickly before their very eyes), this leaves them vulnerable to what we like to call Category Violence: **the relentless exploitation of the incumbent's voluntary immobility.**

One of the most profound shifts happening in the world today is rooted in the ever-escalating debate between generations young and old. It is a shift hiding in plain sight. And just like the Tymshare executives staring out the window at Apple's cranes building the headquarters of the company that would ultimately put them out of business, most people over 35 years old can't see this shift happening.

Instead, they say to themselves, "Eh, we've got nothing to worry about."

Well, as Category Pirates, we feel it is our obligation to sound the alarm when we see rocky shores ahead. Some of us are facing a once-in-a-generation set of headwinds that could not just stymie growth, but sink the entire ship. And if those of us over age 35 aren't careful, this divide could result in one of the greatest instances of Category Neglect and Category Violence we've ever witnessed in human history.

However, those who see this mega shift and act on it, on the other hand, will sail into the sunset a lot of happy pirates, make more money, and make a way bigger difference in the world.

Now, come up on deck, pull up a chair, and let's have a beverage (we have rum, dark rum, and more rum).

A New Category Of Human

There are two types of people on planet earth today.

- **The first are Native Analogs.** These are Baby Boomers and Gen Xers, born anywhere from the 1940s all the way up to the early '80s. Today, they range between the ages of 40 to 75, and make up approximately 136.8 million Americans.
- **The second are Native Digitals.** These are Millennials and Gen Zers, born between the early 1980s to as recently as the 2010s. These demographics are around 35 years of age on the high end today, down to as young as 6 years old, and make up approximately 140.1 million Americans.

The difference?

Native Analogs grew up in a time where technology was an addition, or better yet, a distraction from their real lives.

Native Digitals grew up in a time where their "real" lives

were a distraction from their digital lives.

This is a profound shift—and no one seems to be talking about it. Even more stunning, some of the largest native digital brands on the planet are run by native analogs who don't get it either.

Which is more real: the sunset, or the picture of the sunset?

In early 2021, Pirate Christopher (Native Analog) took a few family members (other Native Analogs) and their kids (Native Digitals) down to the beach in Santa Cruz, California.

"Arrrrr. Let's watch the sunset," he said.

While on the beach, he and the other Native Analogs did what they'd always done: felt the sand between their toes, enjoyed a beverage, had an analog-to-analog conversation while watching the blue sky turn orange. The Native Digitals, on the other hand, did no such thing. They stared at their phones, only looking up long enough to snag a picture of the sky—before spending the rest of the evening Tweeting, Instagramming, and Whatsapping the picture of the sunset to all their (Native Digital) friends.

So, which reality is more real?

The sunset? Or the picture of the sunset?

The answer, fellow pirate, depends entirely on the lens through which you are experiencing life.

If you're a Native Analog, and technology was introduced *in addition to your reality*, you see the sunset as your primary reality and the picture of the sunset as your "virtual"reality."

But if you're a Native Digital, and your reality has always been intertwined with technology, then you see the digital experience of your reality as your primary reality—and everything else as complementary to it.

> *If you're over the age of 35, the above probably sounds like an excerpt out of The Hitchhiker's Guide to the Galaxy. And if you're under the age of 35, the above probably makes complete sense and you're wondering when we're going to stop stating the obvious and get on with it.*

This paradigm shift (Native Analog to Native Digital) is the storm of all storms, the mother of all headwinds (or possibly, the mother of all tailwinds if native analogs woke up)—because we are witnessing a new category of humans emerge for the first time in a long time: a digital-first generation. For example: how are you supposed to come up with an effective marketing strategy if you aren't conscious of whether you are talking to Native Analogs or Native Digitals? And we are noticing that both Native Analog pirates and Native Digital pirates are having a hard time understanding how to take advantage of this unique moment in history.

Why?

Because many Baby Boomers and Gen Xers have (at least a little) contempt for Millennials and Gen Zers (*"What, not enough avocado toast for you?"*).

And many Millennials and Gen Zers have (at least a little) contempt for Baby Boomers and Gen Xers (*"OK Boomer"*).

Most companies today, including the world's largest digital companies, are run by Native Analogs.

- Google CEO, Sundar Pichai, is 49 years old.
- Apple CEO, Tim Cook, is 60 years old.
- Netflix CEO, Reed Hastings, is 60 years old. And Netflix Co-CEO & Chief Content Officer, Ted Sarandos, is 56 years old.
- Amazon CEO, Andy Jassy, is 53 years old. And Amazon Chairman, Jeff Bezos, is 57 years old.
- Even Facebook CEO, Mark Zuckerberg, is just this side of Native Analog. He's 37 years old.

Post coronavirus pandemic, Native Analog CEOs have made it very clear that, from their perspective, they see no reason why employees shouldn't return back to the office (after all, if you're Native Analog, your physical reality is your primary reality). Tim Cook announced employees would be required to return to the office starting in September, 2021; Google, the same. Netflix Co-CEO, Reed Hastings, went so far as to call remote work "a pure negative," insisting all employees must return back to the office as soon as vaccinations have been approved and distributed. (You can hear the contempt in his voice—possibly the same contempt that ended up causing John Antioco to go blind and Blockbuster to go bust? *Careful, Netflix.*)

Well, returning to the office (physical reality being "the primary reality") isn't really what Native Digitals want.

Or, said more specifically, working in a physical office *doesn't make sense to someone whose primary reality is a digital reality. Or to someone (like an introvert, or a J on the Myers Briggs, or the 71%*

of workers who believe meetings are a complete waste of time) who is disengaged from work and sees "virtual work" as a huge work-life balance upgrade.

In response to this insistence to return to the office, Apple employees revolted; as did Google's, prompting one of the largest technology companies in the world to backtrack on its policy and adjust to a hybrid work model where alternating between office work and remote work is allowed. But this is so much more than just a bunch of Millennials whining about wanting to work & eat avocado toast in bed. According to a recent survey by FlexJobs, 58% of workers said they would "absolutely" look for a new job if they could not continue remote work in their current role. And according to Bloomberg, employees would rather quit their jobs than return back to the office.

What native analog CEOs don't seem to realize is that the category of "work" is being redesigned right under their noses *because the category of human is being redesigned under their noses*—and it's going to have a profound impact on their ability to:

- Hire
- Retain talent
- Innovate
- And grow

Especially when Millennials and Gen Zers (native digitals) make up the majority of the workforce. (You now have a 62% chance of reporting to a Millennial boss.)

But if you think "work" (massive, macro category) is as far as this Category Neglect & Category Violence will go, keep reading.

This shift from "Native Analog" to "Native Digital" may impact every category on earth—including one of the largest categories in all of global consumerism:

"Stuff."

Demand for "analog stuff" is falling like a turd from a sailor's ass off the back of a boat.

Native Digitals (Millennials and Gen Zers) don't want "stuff."

This is a profound sea change if you're in the stuff-making business.

Millennials and Gen Z grew up in an era where they watched (at scale through technology and social media) how their parents' pursuit of "stuff" didn't really lead to anything meaningful. Dad's desire to move the family into a bigger house, drive a sports car, and put a big screen TV in the basement didn't make him any happier. Mom's desire to buy diamond necklaces, trendy clothes, and have the newest kitchen appliances didn't make her any more fulfilled. And when grandpa and grandma passed away, and it came time for Mom and Dad to go through their parents' belongings, suddenly the same objects they had once spoken so highly of (antique lamps, silver spoons, and ceramic plates) were referred to as "junk," moved into the garage or the attic.

This is a big deal considering roughly 30% of the U.S. GDP is in the "stuff" business: durable and non-durable goods.

We can see this shift away from valuing "stuff" to valuing digital products, experiences and personal transformation everywhere:

- 74% of Americans now value experiences more than physical products (the majority of which are Millennials)
- Virtual Gucci bags are selling for more than physical Gucci bags (digital goods don't feel like "stuff" since they are infinitely scalable)
- NFTs are indicating what's possible in the new category of digital products
- Cryptocurrencies are becoming a primary "store of value"
- Every client/server enterprise tech company is making the transition to the cloud

For context, 70% of Millennials aren't in a financial position to buy a house, even if they wanted to. (Which means they have nowhere to put their "stuff.") Younger generations aren't even prioritizing getting their driver's licenses (which means they won't be prioritizing buying cars). And Millennials would rather travel and have autonomy over their schedule than land a high-paying job.

Times are a-changin'.

- If you're Harley Davidson and you're in the "analog motorcycle" business, you're in trouble.
- If you're Canon and you're in the "just a camera" business, you're in trouble.
- If you're Nike and you're not leading in the digital sports products category (sneakers are already a goldmine, why

can't the "original" sneaker be a digital copy you carry in your phone?), you're in trouble.
- If you're Costco and you're not relevant in the digital consumer products category (whatever that will mean?), you're in trouble.

The result of this macro trend (happening in plain sight) is that if you are 35 years old or younger, you will progressively spend more time, energy, and money enhancing yourself (through products, experiences, and transformations) in your **digital life** than you will in your analog life.

Consequently, goods (as we know them today) as a percentage of GDP will continue to decline.

Which means, if you're in the 30% of the U.S. GDP in the "stuff-making" business, you should consider the following:

1. Categories that make "stuff" need to innovate digital products and services to go along with their physical products.

Per the World Bank, the global GDP has shifted from 54% services in 1996 to 65% in 2018.

Goods are giving way to services, digital products, experiences and other "non-stuff" sectors.

Apple Care with the iPhone is a great example. IBM moving from physical mainframes and laptops to global software services is another. Specialized transforming bikes into rolling data centers (Like Tesla had done with cars) is a third. These companies understand that digital products and services play a much bigger role in long-term customer loyalty than even the products themselves (and services make up a considerably larger portion of the GDP).

In many cases, this opens the door to transform your offering into "XYZ as a service." Meal kit companies like Hello Fresh are "groceries as a service." Furniture rental companies like Fernish are "interior design & furniture buying as a service." R. "Ray" Wang's new book, *Everybody Wants To Rule The World*, lays out ideas for "home products (think appliances, TVs etc.) as a service" that would radically transform major hard goods categories.

2. Categories/companies that play in a single part of the value chain need to find ways to be more vertically integrated with the end customer.

Selling direct to the consumer is a great way to create "experiences" that differentiate the "stuff" you make.

For example, when you buy a Tesla and it (magically) shows up in your driveway, that is Tesla making the conscious decision to own the final moment of product delivery—opposed to doing what most car manufacturers do, which is sell their cars to third-party dealers and let you spend three hours haggling with them.

Or, when you buy a stock inside Robinhood and your screen explodes in digital confetti, that is Robinhood choosing to own the final moment of product delivery—opposed to doing what most brokerages and financial advisors did in years past, which is say (in a monotone voice), "Alright Bob, looks like your order went through." They turned one of the most boring moments in retail trading into a celebration for the end user.

3. Every part of the customer journey needs to be presented with a little "theatre."

Companies should take a page out of Joe Pine's book, The Experience Economy, and consider how their products can become experiences—and how those experiences can lead to transformations for the customer.

Why does Apple take its products and package them as if they were delivering an Audemars Piguet timepiece? It's theatre.

Why do Southwest flight attendants sing songs and tell jokes? It's theatre.

How come buying something on eBay through an auction is called, "Winning"? It's theatre.

Companies that feel like "more than stuff" are businesses that weave theatre into every function—including sales, customer service & support, and any other interaction that touches the customer experience. Theatre is the reason Eargo is an $80M hearing aid business worth $1.5 billion. Their direct to consumer sales team (made up of trained audiologists) help customers post-sale in empathetic, engaging, and encouraging ways because they know "theatre" is an important part of helping consumers come to grips with the fact they are experiencing hearing loss.

Without this theatre, experience, and transformation in the customer, Eargo would be nothing more than a product company that made "ear stuff."

4. Reimagine the concept of ownership based on the tailwind and customer desire to rent.

Millennials and Gen Zers don't want to buy "stuff."

But they'll happily rent it.

Companies like 1-800-GOT-JUNK have been built (to incredible success) based on the fact that Americans are pack rats and will literally pay someone to show up, on command, and help them get rid of their stuff. "Too much junk" was the same premise that built eBay in the '90s and 2000s, and is the same reason people are opting to sell their cars (or not even bother buying a beater in the first place) and just use Uber to get around instead.

If you are a Native Analog and can take a step back, you may discover your product and business has even more potential if the customer can rent it instead of owning it.

5. Create a portfolio of in-person goods/services/experiences AND virtual goods/services/experiences.

Peloton's portfolio includes a physical bike and screen, connected to an app that guides you through yoga (which has nothing to do with the bike).

So, is Peloton an analog company? Or a digital company?

The answer is yes.

Lululemon's acquisition of Mirror is another great example of a portfolio made of goods (clothing), in-person services/experiences (retail stores), and virtual/digital services (Mirror). Tesla has done this as well, with goods (cars), in-person services (retail stores), in-person services (contactless delivery), and virtual/digital experiences (gaming & premium connectivity).

Domino's is a lesser-known example, as they've invested heavily in technology to build their portfolio of goods (pizza), in-person services/experiences (delivery) and virtual/digital experiences (an app that shows the progress of the pizza: being made, leaving the store, and where it is on the map en route).

All of this explains why a company like Amazon is investing so heavily in content (recently acquiring MGM for $8.45 billion). It's those virtual/digital experiences that keep consumers sticky to Prime.

Questioning the "place" where digital and analog could meet in the context of your category is a smart place to park your brain for a while.

The big takeaway here is that the economics of digital goods are much greater than physical goods.

That's because digital businesses have "increasing returns" business models.

A BIG ah-ha here is in the analog world, costs are pegged to sales. If Starbucks wants to grow, they need to build stores. Physical buildings. Whereas the cost for eBay to serve 10 customers or 10,000 customers is incremental. That's what makes digital businesses *increasing-returns businesses.*

CFOs, take note: digital/virtual goods tend to have much higher LTV because they last "forever." A piece of content like *Friends* can be enjoyed by multiple generations. Peloton's tracker of how many total rides you've done is a badge of honor that grows with value over time (and makes you want to keep going so you don't lose your streak). Perhaps the greatest example of this is the innovation of the frequent flyer program. Airlines are an in-person service/experience. But during the pandemic, United, Delta, and American all took out debt backed by their frequent flyer programs—**and the banks valued the FF programs almost more than the respective airline businesses.**

Why?

Because these programs are fundamentally more profitable, and require far fewer assets to run. In fact, frequent flyer miles might be one of the earliest digital/virtual experiences/services/currencies to be created!

One last story before we let you go.

Let's play out the future where digital goods, services, and experiences become the dominant reality.

De Beers & The Wedding Ring

In 1947, diamond manufacturing company, De Beers deployed one of the most successful category designs and culture-shifting advertising campaigns of all time with the tagline, "A diamond is forever."

This campaign eventually evolved into commercials in the late 1970s where De Beers, quite literally, *defines how much a man should spend on an engagement ring for their significant other.* "How else could two months' salary last forever? A diamond is forever." To this day, ask your friend how much you should spend on a ring, and they'll say, "Well the standard is two months salary." (A more legendary job of category value creation the world has never seen, matey!)

Prior to this campaign, in the 1930s, diamond engagement rings were not the norm or anywhere near as expected as they are today. In fact, only 10% of first-time brides in the '30s and '40s received diamond engagement rings. By 1990, that number was 80%. And between 1939 and 1979, De Beers' wholesale diamond sales in the US grew from $23 million to $2.1 billion.

Said differently: in a world of native analogs valuing physical "stuff," De Beers successfully changed the perceived value of a diamond ring to the tune of two billion dollars. A year.

Great job.

But…

What happens to De Beers in a world that stops valuing "stuff" like diamond rings, gold watches, and gas guzzling automobiles?

Choosing your life partner is one of the most important decisions a human can make in his, her, or their lifetime.

Well, in today's day and age, more than a third of the people in the United States now meet their spouse or partner through their digital life, first. Meanwhile, all the "old ways" you used to meet a suitable mate in the analog world—through friends, at work, or at a bar and restaurant—are falling off a cliff. Today, teenagers and twentysomethings need to do no such things. Your ability to text and get creative with emojis is what determines your success in the dating world.

No copulation without digitization.

To play out how this macro category trend might play out for a company like De Beers, us Pirates decided to play The Breakthrough Game with the legacy category queen to help them look at the world (and more specifically, their business) through the lens of a native digital.

Dear De Beers executives, here's some advice (we know you won't take).

After much *__wipes mouth of rum__* surveying the market, we have come *__hiccup__* to a few conclusions.

The next generation doesn't want your rings. Diamond rings are too expensive, easy to lose, and at risk of being stolen. Diamond rings can break. Rust. They're small, and so even if you take it off your finger for just a second, you'll probably lose it. And diamond rings actually don't last forever. After a generation or two, the ring that used to belong to Great Grandma doesn't have any more sentimental value.

In fact, a physical diamond ring is more annoying than it is valuable, and more of a liability than an asset.

So, here's what we propose you do.

You've already doubled-down on lab-grown synthetic diamonds.*__Holds up pint of rum__* Terrific job, mateys. Now, we can assume other diamond manufacturers will soon follow suit, which means in order to remain category king, you must define the new rules of the new game. Many will produce synthetic diamonds, but you have the opportunity to create "authentic" synthetic diamonds (new category, stay with us). This is step one.

Step two is to treat the digital version of the ring as the __primary product__, and the physical version of the ring as the secondary. Analog products that will survive in the future will have digital versions that stand as "the original." (we might be very wrong about this, but what if we're right?)This means the real thing is the digital thing, and the physical thing is the copy. Who cares if you lose your engagement ring? You just *__hiccup__* 3D print another, and have the customer pay a modest replacement fee. Or, even better, waive the replacement fee—let them lose as many engagement rings as *they want—but charge them $9.99 per month to hold the authentic digital version inside their phone. And let them upgrade to $14.99 per month to hold their husband's digital ring as well, and $29.99 to upload photo albums of historic family moments to embed into the digital DNA of the ring. You want to really make a diamond last forever? Store it in the cloud.*

Oh *wipes mouth of more rum* and while we're on the subject, the reason anyone wants a diamond is sentimental value, and the greatest risk of owning a diamond is destruction. Digital solves for both. Through this lens, an engagement ring is not an engagement ring. It's a time capsule. It's your entire relationship—moments, experiences, transformations in the form of photos and videos and sound clips and GPS tracking your travels around the world, saved inside your phone. After all, getting married is one of the most transformative experiences available to humans. You have the opportunity to represent that transformation. Digitally.

Do this successfully (through a native digital lens), and you become Tesla on your finger.

Don't (through a native analog lens), and you become that old antique piece of jewelry your granddaughter will one day call "a piece of junk."

Marketing Is Not Just About Creative Campaigns

As you've probably gathered so far in this book, our lens on marketing begins with: *what type of human being are you dealing with?* Are they a Native Analog, living in the analog world? Or are they a Native Digital, living in the digital world?

You have to start there, otherwise whatever creative marketing idea you come up with is completely detached from reality.

But, if you can get clear on who exactly your product/service/information is for, then, *then*, your marketing efforts have a shot.

2

The Big Brand Lie

Have you ever met someone who's been drafted into a cult?

Did you know it's possible to be in a cult and not know it?

A meaningful percentage of marketers, entrepreneurs, and executives are in what we like to call "The Brand Cult." They've been taught the best (aka: *"the most well known"*) brand wins.

Even though the data shows this is not true.

- Ford spends $2.5 billion per year on brand advertising, with a market cap of $50 billion. General Motors spends $3 billion, with a market cap of $70 billion. Meanwhile, Tesla spends $0, but has a market cap of $700 billion. *What?!?*
- In 2011, Google spent almost $600 million building and launching a social network to compete with Facebook and Twitter called Google+. If "the best **brand** wins," how come Google+ failed? After all, Forbes named Google the 2nd "most valuable brand in the world" in 2020.
- Comcast spends more than $5 billion on branding and advertising each year. And yet, Comcast has long been

considered "America's Most Hated Company." There's even a Wikipedia page dedicated to the company's inadequacies, titled "Criticism of Comcast." (United Airlines is a close second, if you ask us.) So if branding and "shouting from the rooftops" is the key to winning the game, how come $5 billion per year can't solve Comcast's problems? Maybe they need $10 billion?

But sharing data with a cult member is about the worst thing you can do. That's because facts are upsetting to feelings—particularly facts that disprove everything you've been taught to believe.

Well, here's a fact:

Categories make brands. Not the other way around.

How The Brand Cult Began

In 2011, *The Atlantic* published a piece titled, "How Brands Were Born: A Brief History of Modern Marketing."

> *"In the 1950s, consumer packaged goods companies like Procter and Gamble, General Foods and Unilever developed the discipline of brand management, or marketing as we know it today, when they noticed the quality levels of products being offered by competitors around them improve.* ***A brand manager would be responsible for giving a product an identity that distinguished it from nearly indistinguishable competitors.****"*

Note that last sentence.

From our perspective, the obvious response and *clear* "no brainer" solution to being "nearly indistinguishable" is to get **different**: design a new space, come up with something new, and make others play a game you created.

But that's not what most "marketing & branding experts" decided.

Instead, they said, "Let's ignore the fact there is nothing unique about us, our product, or what we do for the world. Instead, let's do some **branding**." As if sprinkling some kind of magic dust on your "brand" (changing the colors, the font, the logo design, etc.) is going to drive a breakthrough in growth. Or, even worse, "Let's call ourselves a community. Let's use big, all-encompassing, undifferentiated language to make ourselves appeal to everyone. Something like, 'We are an authentic, purpose-driven brand.'"

And thus, "the brand cult" was formed—and The Big Brand Lie began.

"The Room Where It Happened"

We will live the rest of our lives wondering how branding as a solution to a lack of differentiation ever made it out the room ("The room where it happened").

> *"No one else was in the room where it happened, the room where it happened, the room where it happened.*
>
> *No one else was in the room where it happened, the room where it happened, the room where it happened.*

> *No one knows how the game is played, the art of the trade, how the sausage gets made.*
>
> *We just assumed that it happens.*
>
> *But no one else is in the room where it happens."*
>
> –Hamilton, The Musical

And yet, every single day, we are shocked by how many MBAs, entrepreneurs, founders, even very smart investors, accept this premise.

How could the answer to the problem, "We're indistinguishable," possibly be cosmetic attributes?

How could the answer to the problem, "We're the same thing," be, "Let's say we're the same thing, *but better and louder and more often?*"

How could the answer to the problem, "We've run out of ideas," be, "Let's make the logo BIGGER!?"

There are approximately 7,000 books on "branding" on Amazon.

Our guess is that many of them extol the value of "building a brand" as a path to success.

Make The Logo BIGGER!

The "Make the logo BIGGER!" marketing strategy is the opposite of Category Design.

Category Design is the process of moving customers *FROM* the way the world is *TO* a new and different way. Categories are about customers, their problems, their opportunities, and their future—which means **category marketing is about**

educating customers on a new and different solution that unlocks transformational outcomes by solving a specific problem.

Branding, on the other hand, is about us. Our name. Our logo. Our team. Our "mission statement." Which means brand marketing is about screaming, "LOOK AT ME, LOOK AT ME!" Whereas category marketing is about evangelizing a different outcome altogether.

Said differently:

Brand marketing is something we do *to* customers.

Category marketing is something we do **for** customers.

The Story of Ralph Lauren

Ask any person on earth why Ralph Lauren was successful, and 99% of them will say the same thing:

"He built an incredible brand."

But is that actually what *caused* his success? Or was the Ralph Lauren brand the result of his creating a DIFFERENT category?

If you haven't seen the documentary on Ralph Lauren, called *Very Ralph*, we highly recommend it.

Most people don't know that Ralph Lauren is credited with creating the menswear industry as "a designer reality." In the 1960s, men had gotten used to prescriptive dressing, and wore suits as uniforms with very little differentiation and personality. "Designers were for the women. The tailor was for men." Lauren was the first designer to turn American "lifestyle" moments and characters (a carpenter, a railroad worker, a cowboy) into fashionable everyday looks.

And it all started with his unique "wide" ties.

In the documentary, he tells the story:

> *"I like these ties. I'm going to make them wider. I'm going to bring them over to the store, I think they're going to like it. So I took them over to Bloomingdale's, because Bloomingdale's was the entree into every store—because every store at that time was shopping Bloomingdale's to see what was new. Who were the new resources? What's happening? The buyer looked at the tie and said, 'It's too wide, and would you make it a little narrower, and will you take the label off? We want to have our store brand.'"*

To which Ralph Lauren closed his sample case and walked away—and the rest is history.

The misunderstanding here is that what made Ralph Lauren different from all the other ties in the market was the **brand**, and that's *not* it at all. What made Ralph Lauren ties (the company's first successful product) different was the fact that they were wider. They were the first tie to break the mold of what a tie should look like for men—and the first tie that even remotely resembled having its own distinct style. Ralph's ties were *different*, and as a result, created a new category of *wide designer* ties. The "brand" and the tag simply let people know where they could get more DIFFERENT ties like it.

And in the 1960s, what happens when you wear a wide tie?

Well, you need different shirts, with different collars. You need a different suit. (Remember: new categories create more new categories.) And suddenly, Ralph Lauren was creating a whole new category of menswear. What Lauren was *not* doing was copy/pasting his brand onto similar, commodity products. He was inventing new and DIFFERENT products—which, after the fact, were paired with the Ralph Lauren tag and brand.

Fast-forward to today, and despite the fact that Ralph Lauren will go down in history as one of the greatest fashion designers ever (and the company boasts an $8 billion market cap), it's differentiation strategy today amounts to little other than, "Make the logo BIGGER!"

The Definition Of Branding

But before we go any further, let's think deeply about this word the business world loves so much.

Remember: *thinking about thinking is the most important kind of thinking.*

BRANDING. What did this word originally mean?

It meant "livestock branding."

> *"The practice of branding—in the original literal sense of marketing by burning—is thought to have begun with the ancient Egyptians, who were known to have engaged in livestock branding as early as 2,700 BCE. Branding was used to differentiate one person's cattle from another's by means of a distinctive symbol burned into the animal's skin with a hot branding iron. If a person stole any of the cattle, anyone else who saw the symbol could deduce the actual owner. The term has been extended to mean a strategic personality for a product or company, so that 'brand' now suggests the values and promises that a consumer may perceive and buy into."*

OK, so let's just think about this for a second.

The marketing world thought it would be a good idea to borrow a word that meant "burning a symbol into a cow" to represent the act of claiming customers as your own. *Hmmm....* So branding is a violent, painful approach to showing a living being as belonging to you.

That sounds about right.

Enduring most branding efforts, as a customer, is painful.

- Maybe this this is why advertisers use the term "impressions" as a feeble proxy for a real outcome when selling advertising to corporations?
- Maybe this means brands think of customers as their own property?
- Maybe this is why companies that spend billions of dollars in brand advertising per year also happen to be the companies at the top of the "most-hated" lists?

For example: how many times have you seen a huge Capital One banner ad advertising on a major publication, taking up 50% of the screen?

We bet this big banner ad is getting lots of brand impressions, which means it must be working! Right? Actually, if we sober up for half a second and look, the data shows us it's not. Capital One spent $1.6 billion on advertising in 2020, and has been averaging $1.9 billion per year in ad spend for the past 5 years. And yet, after the stock failed to move from 2015 to 2020, the company authorized a "new share buyback program of up to $7.5 billion for 2021," causing the stock to artificially rise. So basically, $1.6 billion (or more) per year advertising Capital One's brand has done nothing—so much so the company decided to deploy $7.5 billion more in cash to prop up the stock.

Let us really soak in this for a second. Capital One could not drive growth in their value through marketing. So they cooked-up fake growth with stock buybacks. CEOs buying their own stock communicate at least three (horrible) things about the company.

1. They have run out of ideas
2. They are using shareholder's cash, to increase their own stock compensation
3. And worst of all, they have given up trying to increase their value in a real way

Capital One is not alone here. In 2014, HBR published a piece by William Lazonick, a University of Massachusetts professor, called "Profits Without Prosperity." Here he noted 449 companies in the S&P 500 index from 2003 to 2012 used 54% of their earnings to buy back their own stock. Another 37% of earnings were used for dividends, meaning 91% total corporate earnings from the S&P 500 went to buybacks.

Given that stock options and awards comprise the lion share of executive compensation, executives who are stewards are self-dealing at the expense of investing in growth. Stock buybacks plus stock-based compensation at slow growth companies is one of the single greatest examples of 'legal larceny' committed in plain sight.

Now, we didn't get invited to the Marketing Leadership Council meeting where "marketing experts" decided "branding" and "brand advertising" was the best way to spend a billion dollars per year. Had we been invited, we would have slammed our mugs down on the table and shouted, "That's a chantey without a clap o' thunder down from Davy Jones' locker if we ever heard it!" *(If you are still learning to speak Pirate, that means we think "branding" is a horrible name and makes absolutely no sense.)*

Are we being cheeky?

No. THINK.

Branding is defined as **burning your name on someone to claim ownership.**

Imagine branding as an idea doesn't exist. Imagine you're a marketing executive at Procter & Gamble and the guy next to you is saying, "Man, everybody's detergent is the same. What do we do? Wait, I know. Let's make it look different. Let's give it a different identity. Let's make it stand out by giving it unique colors on the box." This is what eventually becomes "branding" (as a multibillion-dollar industry) and NOBODY goes, "Wait, hang on a minute. Maybe the solution to the problem, 'We're not different,' is to actually *get* different—not just try to dress ourselves up as different."

But this is what brand marketers do. Their entire job is predicated on their ability to burn their company's name and logo into the minds and bodies of their customers. Success is then measured by how many people they *believe* they've prodded with a hot poker (example: Capital One). *"Congratulations! This month we reached a new high score of X million impressions. We believe we branded them—therefore, we did brand them. Keep buying more branding efforts!"*

Smooth Brain Brand Plus

There's a term that rumbles in the underbelly of the Internet (also known as Reddit) that represents people who can't think for themselves.

"Smooth brained apes."

> *"One of the first things people notice about the human brain is its intricate landscape of hills and valleys. These convolutions derive from the cerebral cortex, a two- to four-millimeter-thick mantle of gelatinous tissue packed with neurons sometimes called gray matter that mediates our perceptions, thoughts, emotions and actions. Other large-brained mammals such as whales, dogs and our great ape cousins have a corrugated cortex, too each with its own characteristic pattern of convolutions. **But small-brained mammals and other vertebrates have relatively smooth brains.**"* —Scientific American

Well, one of the *smoothest brain brand strategies* in marketing today is to take your brand and then slap it on anything and everything you can find. Because the brand is what made you successful, right? Brands drive growth, right? Everybody knows how important branding is! The brand is what people love!

In 1994 (so ahead of their time), Al Ries & Jack Trout wrote one of the definitive books on "business thinking," *The 22 Immutable Laws Of Marketing.* And in Chapter 18, The Law of Success, they state the following:

> *"Success is often the fatal element behind the rash of line extensions. When a brand is successful, the company assumes the name is the primary reason for the brand's success. So they promptly look for other products to plaster the name on. Actually, it's the opposite. The name didn't make the brand famous (although a bad name might keep the brand from becoming famous.) The brand got famous because you made the right marketing moves. In other words, the steps you took were in tune with the fundamental laws of marketing. You got into the mind first. You narrowed the focus. You preempted a powerful attribute. Your success puffs up your ego to such an extent that you put the famous name on other products. Result: early success and long-term failure...".*

If blindly branding customers with a hot poker is mistake numero uno, then mistake number dos is taking your brand and doing what Ries & Trout famously languaged as "line extension": taking your brand and *extending* it across multiple categories.

- Disney+
- Apple TV+
- ESPN+
- Hulu+
- Samsung TV+
- BET+
- Paramount+

Did we learn nothing from Google+?

Here's how this stupidity gets rationalized.

In 2020, *FastCompany* (a commodity, undifferentiated business "brand") published a piece titled, "Why adding 'Plus' to the name of every streaming service is actually good." In it, ViacomCBS president and CEO, Bob Bakish, explains, "Paramount is an iconic and storied **brand** beloved by consumers all over the world, and it is synonymous with quality, integrity, and world-class storytelling."

> *Pause.*
> *Real quick, name one Paramount film.*
> *Just one.*
> *If Paramount is SUCH an iconic brand, and branding is all that matters, then surely you can remember which films Paramount has made versus which films 21st Century Fox has made, versus Universal Pictures, versus Columbia Pictures, right?*
> *Can't?*
> *Moving on.*

Bakish continues, "With Paramount Plus, we're excited to establish one global streaming brand in the broad-pay segment that will draw on the sheer breadth and depth of ViacomCBS portfolio to offer an extraordinary collection of content for everyone to enjoy."

Let's go back to how we started this chapter, and the origin of branding: ***"A brand manager would be responsible for giving a product an identity that distinguished it from nearly*** *indistinguishable competitors."*

Whether Bob Bakish realizes it or not, he is explicitly announcing to the world that Paramount Plus is no different from any of its competitors. The only difference is that its catalog of products (and by extension, it's viewers) have been "branded" with the Paramount logo. (A brand who is so "iconic," no one can name a single one of their movies.)

The (rocket-surgeon) author of the *FastCompany* article then goes on to explain, "Ahhh, but there is a method to all this Plus madness. What if it was all designed to make our lives less confusing?" **Listen to the words.**

Translation: The reason a big brand like Paramount decides to use "Plus" to describe its new product offering is because executives (and *FastCompany* writers) believe you are too "smooth brained" to understand anything different. If they DIDN'T call it Paramount Plus, how would you possibly find the content you were searching for?

The article then closes out the argument with a quote from the Chief Creative Officer of Initial, Initial & Initial, "It's such a complex landscape out there for consumers. There's so much content, so much choice, so many different layers of everything. I think brands have sort of banded together with these signifiers to make it easier for people to peg what kind of product it is."

Listen. To. The. Words.

- "We think fitting in (not differentiating) is a wise growth strategy."
- "You are too dumb to figure out what you want to watch on your own."

- "Your content preferences aren't relevant. You will blindly follow whichever logo is the biggest (SING IT..."Make the logo BIGGER!")."
- "Today's media landscape is so big, and so complex, that the best path forward is for brands to all use the same signifiers so that *products can be more easily compared against each other.*"

Bob Bakish, *FastCompany*, and most Chief Creative Officers, are all premium members of "The Brand Cult."

Unfortunately, this sort of comparison marketing leads nowhere except "The Better Trap."

And companies that fall into "The Better Trap" all fight for 24% (minority share) of the category.

A few other great examples of how "line extension" never works:

Red Bull Cola

In 2008, on the heels of Red Bull's meteoric rise creating the "energy drink" category, the company decided it was time to broaden their horizons. Unfortunately, instead of creating a new category, the company decided to take its brand and try to extend it into another already established category: Cola.

At the time, Red Bull UK's managing director said in a press release, "The new product will benefit from full integration into Red Bull's brand marketing initiatives, sitting alongside Red Bull energy drink." Well, if Red Bull was one of the most recognizable brands in the world, and if brand marketing is so successful, why did Red Bull pull the plug (along with its other "line extension" product, Red Bull Energy Shots) three years later? Because Coke owns the Cola category, and 5-Hour Energy owns the Energy Shot category—and you will never overthrow the category leader by extending your brand into someone else's category.

We find it stunning how some of the greatest category creators *ever* forget what made them successful. **Categories are about customers. Brands are about us.** We're not shrinks, shamans, or doctors of any kind, but we do suspect this has to do with the human ego. We want to believe *we* make us successful. When the truth is, customers make us successful.

Categories make brands. Not the other way around.

The Microsoft Store

In 2009, another one of the most well-known brands and most valuable companies in the world, Microsoft, decided to take on Apple's legendary in-store customer experience by launching The Microsoft Store.

"We want to showcase what's possible with the full Microsoft brand," said David Porter, corporate VP of Microsoft Retail, in a press release promoting the launch.

By 2015, the company announced, "Today, more than 80 percent of Americans live within 20 miles of a Microsoft store, with more than 110 stores across the U.S., Puerto Rico and Canada."

Fast-forward to 2020, and Microsoft decided to shut the doors on the operation, "resulting in a pre-tax charge of approximately $450 million," according to CNBC. That's half a billion dollars spent trying to extend their brand into Apple's category. "Microsoft even built a store on 5th Avenue in New York City, just blocks away from Apple's iconic glass cube store."

Line extension doesn't work.

You can't take your brand and stroll up into someone else's category.

And yet, executives at some of the most legendary companies in the world—companies that, at one point, designed and dominated massive categories—continue to spread the gospel of "The Brand Cult."

Trillions in market cap has been destroyed with these asinine branding "strategies."

And trillions more will be.

Your New Role As CMO: Prepare 3 Envelopes

Success in most marketing roles means changing jobs every 18-36 months.

That's how you know you're climbing the ladder.

Especially in Fortune 500 companies, the pattern is as follows:

- **First 6 months:** Dump on the person before you ("They did it all wrong").
- **Next 6 months:** "Make The Logo BIGGER!"
- **Final 6 months:** Move onto your next gig.

Let us show you how this works by telling you a short Pirate fable.

You're the new CMO. Congrats!

The old CMO says, "I wish you all the success in the world. Good luck. And to help you out, I've left 3 envelopes on my desk with some advice—in case you ever need it."

So, you get settled. You move into your new office. But then after the welcome parties simmer down, and your responsibilities pick up speed, people start asking questions. "What are you contributing to revenue? What's our ROI? How do we know we are gaining market share?" Turns out, being a CMO is hard! *A bit harder than things seemed in the job description.*

You aren't sure how to handle things, so you open Envelope #1.

You pull out a sheet of paper, and all it says is one word:
"Rebrand."
Terrific idea! Branding is the solution to everything.
So, you put together a fancy PowerPoint presentation. You call all the other executives into a meeting. And you say, "Listen. Growth isn't where we want it to be. We're not distinguished from our competitors. We need a rebrand." And all the smooth-brained executives start nodding their heads, *Yes... Yes...*

> *Note: If a company hires a new CMO and rebrands within the first 12 months, quit or sell the stock. You're screwed.*

The good news is, most rebranding initiatives take anywhere from 8 to 24 months to complete. Anytime someone asks you what you're doing or why the company's marketing isn't yielding meaningful results, all you have to say is, "That's because we're in the middle of a rebrand." Ah, OK. Got it.

Fast-forward a year, and the rebrand is done. You have a brand new shiny logo. Can't you tell the difference?

(Probably not.)

For a while, everyone on the team is ecstatic. "I LOVE THE COLORS!" It's practically a work of art. (Meanwhile, Andy Warhol is rolling in his grave.) Until a few months pass and people start asking questions. "Did the rebrand work? Is revenue up? Have our competitors waved the white flag yet?" The questions won't stop!

In a jam, you open Envelope #2.

"Re-org."

An amazing idea!

You start to think about it, and of course it makes sense why the rebrand didn't change the company's position in the marketplace. Just look around! The office is a disaster—nobody knows how to communicate with anybody. It's time to move from a centralized model to a decentralized model. (Because if you're not the category leader, you're fighting for just 24% of the value in the category. So you can position, reposition, brand, and rebrand all you want, but growth will be very hard.)

"How long will it take?" another executive asks.

"Probably 12 to 18 months," you say, shaking your head. "It's going to be tough, but we have to do it."

And off the company goes, rebranding and re-orging.

Until finally, after you've been with the company for a little over two years, you realize things aren't going anywhere. "It's time for me to jump ship," you say over drinks with an executive at another company. When you return back to the office, people won't leave you alone. More questions, always more questions. "Did the rebrand work? Did the re-org work?" You've had enough. Clearly, nobody onboard is up to your caliber of talent! And so you open the last envelope, hoping for some parting advice from the previous CMO.

You open it up, pull out the sheet of paper, and it says…

"Prepare three envelopes."

The Role Brands Should Play In Category Design

If brand marketing doesn't work, then what's a marketer, an executive, an entrepreneur to do?

The answer is certainly not to come up with airy-fairy attributes and qualities in an attempt to "distinguish" the company, product, or service from identical offerings ("Make the logo BIGGER!").

The only time you should ever re-brand is when you are launching a new category design.

However, branding in the absence of category design is asinine.

Remember: categories make brands, not the other way around.

Google's brand is only valuable **in the context of the category it created and dominated**, which is Search. Take Google's brand and extend it into Facebook's "social network" category, and it's worthless (Google+). Same goes for Microsoft and it's attempt to extend its brand into Apple's category of in-store experiences.

Instead, branding should be used in conjunction *with the new and different category you are creating.* The category and brand have to come together in some meaningful way for the customer, consumer, or user.

For example:

- **Barcade: The original Arcade Bar.** It's not a bar, and it's not an arcade. It's an Arcade Bar. It's a different thing, in a different category. The brand then reflects all the things that make this thing fundamentally different.
- **5-Hour Energy: Energy shots.** The category is "energy shots." And the brand is "5-hour Energy." The brand name reflects the differentiated category. The two are inextricably linked.
- **Under Armour: Athletic undergarments.** The category is, "clothes you wear under your clothes when you're being athletic." And the brand is, "Under Armour." The brand name is telling customers what the category is. "Under Armour is the originator of performance apparel—sportswear engineered to keep athletes cool, dry and light throughout the course of a game, practice, or workout." Their brand, in the context of this new and different category they created, is legendary. Outside of this category, Under Armour is a next-next-next-best alternative to Nike, Adidas, and so on.
- **Amazon.com: e-Commerce.** Amazon was the first company of consequence to put *dot com* in their name. This immediately communicated that Amazon was radically different from any other "bookstore." And it's tagline in the beginning screamed their digital difference. "The Earth's Biggest Bookstore." (Thousands of companies followed in their footsteps and realized, "Hey, if we put *dot com* in our name, we'll be valued as a futuristic e-Commerce company

too.")

When done successfully, your company's branding efforts do not (just) create the style guide for your company, *but the style guide for the category.* You can see this happening in plain sight when competitors start:

- Talking like you
- Looking like you
- Using similar features as you

All of which makes the category bigger (of which you, as the category leader, will capture the lion's share of the economics).

Most small 'e' entrepreneurs intuitively understand branding hierarchy in category design.

Whereas most MBAs from Ivy League schools (wearing pleated pants and blue button-downs) do not.

For proof, look at any local sign for a dentist.

- **BIG FONT:** DENTIST
- ***Small font:*** *Mark Johnson, DDS.*

Or, how about your local landscaping company?

- **BIG FONT:** LANDSCAPING
- ***Small font:*** *Miller's Landscaping Since 1992*

Or how about your plumber? What does the side of their truck say?

- **BIG FONT:** PLUMBER
- ***Small font:*** *O'Connor Plumbing. Call us today!*

Category first, brand second.

Because if we are plumbers, and we say, "Hey you should really call Eddie, Cole, and Christopher," you don't care. You don't have a clue what we're talking about. Are we plumbers? Are we fast-food delivery guys? Are we landscapers? You need to know what *category of thing* we are, first. Then, once you understand the category, you start searching for the "best brand" within that category.

Big 'E' Entrepreneurs, on the other hand, have a much harder time keeping their ego in check.

It's as if the moment your startup passes $100 million in funding you blackout and forget what made you successful wasn't your brand, your logo, your name, or even you and your incredible track record as an entrepreneur.

What made you successful was your ability to create a new and differentiated *category* of product, service, or offering—to which your brand name just happened to be attached.

Again: Ralph Lauren's brand isn't what made his "wide ties" successful.

His new and differentiated category of product, "wide ties," were successful, which made his brand successful as a result.

Force A Choice. Don't Invite A Comparison

So, if you are an entrepreneur, an executive, or a marketer, we urge you to ask this very important question:

What are you DOING with your marketing?

Are you forcing a choice? *"We are a different thing altogether."*

Or are you inviting a comparison? *"We're like everybody else, PLUS some more!"* Or *"We're like everybody else, MINUS the bad stuff!"*

The answer to this question is the seminal difference between brand marketing and category marketing.

Somehow, the business world got duped into solving a problem called, "We're not different," by putting drapes on the painting—opposed to creating a different painting.

Stop arguing over whose drapes are the best.

Paint a different painting.

3

The "Better" Trap

Let's do a little exercise.

We want you to think about anything you want except pink unicorns.

No pink unicorns, that's the only rule. You can think about anything, anything in the whole wide world, just not pink unicorns. You can think about lions. Zebras. Giraffes. The entire Amazon forest, if you'd like. Just absolutely, under no circumstances, can you think about pink unicorns.

Now, Pirate....
What are you thinking about?
PINK UNICORNS!

The Pepsi (Pink Unicorn) Challenge

In 1975, Pepsi ran what many marketers (mistakenly) believe to be one of the most "creative" marketing campaigns in history.

The challenge consisted of a single blind taste test.

Pepsi representatives would stop unknowing customers

at malls, shopping centers, and other public places and ask them to take a sip of two identical looking cups of cola: one containing Coke, the other Pepsi. The results were then compiled into TV advertising campaigns aimed to convince the general public that more Americans preferred the taste of Pepsi to Coke.

Now, let's do the same exercise again.

We want you to think about anything you want except Coca-Cola. No Coca-Cola, that's the only rule. You can think about anything, anything in the whole wide world, just not Coca-Cola.

Now, Pirate…

What are you thinking about?

COCA-COLA!

Legendary writer, Malcolm Gladwell, debunked the "success" of the Pepsi challenge 30 years later in his book, *Blink*. According to Gladwell, the same people who say in a blind taste test they prefer Pepsi because of its sweetness don't end up finishing a whole can because they find it *too sweet*. But nevermind that.

For more than 100 years, Pepsi's entire marketing strategy has been in comparison to the category king of soda: Coca-Cola. There is almost no finer example than the very first line of dialogue in Pepsi's Super Bowl LIII commercial in 2020, broadcasted to 4 million people (and viewed who-knows-how-many-millions-of-times online thereafter).

"I'll take a Coke."

Pepsi might as well Venmo its entire marketing budget to The Coca-Cola Company.

Why?

Because according to our research, Category Kings capture the lion's share of the upside of the category. More importantly, for every $1.00 of revenue growth, category creators generate $4.82 of market cap growth (compared to $1.77 generated for other fast-growing companies).

Over the past 10 to 20 years, has Pepsi's "better product" marketing strategy been working?

No.

If anything, it has further reinforced the fact that Coca-Cola is the king of the soda category. Pepsi's market share has been falling for more than a decade—which means, despite the company spending tens of millions of dollars on Super Bowl ads (or enlisting social media stars like Kendall Jenner to represent the brand), these efforts haven't had any meaningful impact on dethroning Coca-Cola's leadership position.

According to Nielsen (one of the global leaders in marketing mix modeling), the average dollar spent on advertising brings in only $0.70 of gross profit. This insight was derived from 40,000+ marketing mix models across hundreds of categories, all over the world. The takeaway here is that most companies would be more profitable (or, in Pepsi's case, just as good of a "sweeter" category alternative) if they spent nothing on marketing at all.

For example, Pepsi's market share in 1984 was 18.8%.

In 2009, Pepsi's market share was down to 10%.

Then, in 2018, it was 8.4%.

In 2018, Pepsico spent $118 million dollars on advertising

Pepsi, down from $139 million in 2013. Let's make the conservative assumption that Pepsi has spent at least $100 million dollars per year on advertising the Pepsi brand since 1984. **That adds up to $3.6 billion dollars.** Factoring in inflation and nominal returns from investing in treasuries, let's call this $5 billion dollars. So per Nielsen, if Pepsi was "average" in its marketing ROI, they returned $3.5 billion back in gross profits on their $5 billion in advertising.

We'd bet the ROI was even lower given a) all this money was spent on comparison marketing, b) soda as a category has been in decline for more than a decade and c) new beverage categories have risen dramatically in coffee (Starbucks, Keurig, Nespresso), energy drinks (Red Bull, Monster, 5-Hour Energy) and so forth.

Comparison marketing isn't just bad marketing. It's bad business strategy.

Strategy is often defined as how you allocate scarce resources to achieve the highest return on investment. So the question is: what else could Pepsi have done with $5 billion dollars to get a higher return?

To find our answer, let's play the "What if I was a Category Pirate?" game.

What if, instead of paying Cardi B to yell *OKURRRRRR* in a Super Bowl ad, Pepsi used all that wasted advertising money and bought a company that yielded a breakthrough business model and a breakthrough data flywheel?

Pepsi could have bought:

1. **Green Mountain Coffee Roasters for $2.5 billion in 2009.** This would be 3 years after Green Mountain acquired Keurig, becoming one of the great category creators in coffee. Pepsi then would have had instant distribution into offices (one of the great hidden gems of a direct-to-consumer business), leapfrogging Coke's "within an arm's reach" strategy. Coffee palates are also highly predictive of broader beverage palates, so this would have been an amazing data flywheel for Pepsi. (Green Mountain Keurig would later go private for $13.9 billion. Whoops.)
2. **Domino's Pizza for $1.7 billion dollars in 2005.** Pizza is a great business on its own, but it would have given Pepsi yet another hugely strategic distribution arm with delivery drivers all over the US—who could have easily added on a 2-liter of Pepsi and bags of Frito-Lay salty snacks as upsells to every order. Pepsi would have also had access to a burgeoning tech company, Domino's being one of the leaders in testing self-driving cars for delivery. (Domino's market cap today is $17 billion dollars. Whoops.)

We can go on and on.

Both ideas are powerful because they would have given Pepsi a) a new category, b) new business models and distribution, and c) an amazing data flywheel. Pepsi (and Coke) spend 9-10 figures per year on consumer data. And yet all they really understand is the purchasing behaviors of their distributors, retailer customers, and food service customers. But they don't have any direct-to-consumer information of consequence.

The devil's advocate argument here is always, "We would have lost more money if we didn't advertise the Pepsi brand" or "hindsight is 20/20." But again we ask, what is the point of doing the worst kind of marketing there is (comparison marketing) **in a declining category** with a brand/product that likely already has 100% awareness and is no different than it was from before?

If you hold up comparison marketing (which is most of marketing) against a true business strategy lens and instead ask, "Can we generate a higher return elsewhere?" then you get a very different picture.

Most marketers and entrepreneurs spend their entire careers competing for only 24% of the value opportunity of the category.

And just like Pepsi, they don't even know it.

Our research shows the Category King earns 76% of the category's total value, meaning everyone else is left to fight over the remaining 24%. Within that remaining 24% is a barrel of brands all trying to "out-better" each other. *"We're cheaper! We're faster! We've got this feature! We're free for 30 days! We're free for 31 days!"* And so on.

But the moment you decide—or, to say it more accurately, *the moment you make the unconscious, unquestioned, unconsidered, undiscussed decision*—to compete with a "better marketing / product" strategy, what you're really doing is competing for table scraps.

You are quietly admitting defeat, and announcing to the world you would be satisfied with second place.

Because your entire existence is rooted ***in the context of someone else.***

Here's another example of the "better product" strategy in action: In 2020, we saw a billboard by a new company called Whereby that said, "The *New York Times* says we do video meetings better than Zoom."

Ask any run-of-the-mill marketer what they think of this billboard, and they'll likely say the following:

- "It's so creative."
- "I love the font."
- "It looks sleek and modern."
- "*The New York Times*? Amazing testimonial!"

(Pirate Christopher actually read these comments on a marketing community site, and we curated them here for your enjoyment.)

But ask these marketers if they, themselves, have switched from Zoom to using this "new, better" product called Whereby, and they'll all say the same thing.

"No."

Whereby attacks Zoom head-on.

Zoom doesn't even acknowledge Whereby's existence.

Which one do you perceive to be the leader?

"Better" is a trap.

Even the world's most successful, most legendary category designers make this mistake.

- Google thought they could build a "better" social network than Facebook called Google+ (which became known as a

"sad, expensive failure").
- Microsoft thought they could build a "better" in-store experience than Apple (which resulted in $450 million in losses on the company's balance sheet).

What's really happening here is the company is making the *unconscious, unquestioned, unconsidered, undiscussed decision* to carry their brand into someone else's category and try to convince the world that their product is "better." It happens all the time. And it's always a disaster. But so many people have been recruited into the "better" product cult and "better" brand cult, this behavior will likely continue—probably for the rest of time.

Anytime a company makes a comparison statement, they are falling into the "better" trap.

Here are some easy-to-spot examples:

- Faster (faster than…what?)
- Smarter (smarter than…what?)
- Cheaper (cheaper than…what?)
- More economical (more economical than…what?)
- Most efficient (most efficient compared to…what?)

Words that end in -er and "most/more-than" statements imply comparison. Because in order for something to be fast-*er* or smart-*er* or cheap-*er*, something else has to exist to give it meaning.

Category designers, on the other hand, focus on creating a **different** future. The need to draw a product / feature comparison is irrelevant.

The way the world understands business strategy is the problem.

Strategy isn't about "better" vs" worse." It's not about competition.

Strategy is about finding ways to be different (which is not the same as, "We do this one feature 'better' than our competitors, and that's what makes us different.").

When MBAs and management consultants do what they call "strategy," it is really just "competitive strategy," which is a subset of true business strategy. What they're doing is throwing their category lens out the window and evaluating companies in the context of 1) the past and 2) the competition (in the past). It's a conversation around features, capabilities, and price (aka value) ***the competition*** *has been able to extract historically.*

Category designers, on the other hand, focus on creating net-new potential.

Instead of having a conversation about the past, you have a conversation with your customers and investors about the future—specifically, the future potential of the category. For example, Elon Musk doesn't talk about Tesla in the context of gasoline-powered engines, American car manufacturers, and legacy brands. He talks about Tesla in the future: a world where gasoline doesn't exist and clean energy saves our planet.

So, what's the value of Tesla?

- If you valued the company through the lens of Ford's historical performance, you were probably one of the many investors who lost their shorts shorting Tesla stock.
- And if you valued the company through a category lens focused on future category potential, you were probably one of the many retail investors who became a Tesla

millionaire.

Don't be "Better." Be DIFFERENT!

When most people say "marketing," what they mean is the following:

"We're going to launch a product or service in an existing market category, and then we're going to market why ours is better than the competition. Once the world sees that we're better, they'll stop buying from the current Category Queen and start buying from us."

But when this is your business and marketing strategy, all you're really doing is educating customers on who the real Category Queen is (hint: it's not you) and Venmoing that company your marketing budget.

Because they're the ones who capture the majority of the category's upside—not you.

This "strategy" (if we can even call it that) leads you into a never-ending competition (with all the other slum lords competing for 24% of the category's remaining value) over ***features***. There's just one problem: any feature that allows you to "win" will only last for a short period of time—because any feature you can come up with, so can the Category Queen (remember when Snapchat created the Stories feature, and then Instagram copied it?).

The unfortunate result of all this absent-minded behavior is an erosion of the category's value as a whole—and more specifically, your company's margins.

> *We think it's important to note that "better" is often associated with something that is more incremental than*

> *exponential. And now is arguably the greatest time in history to be working on the exponential. (We're not devaluing the important role ongoing improvements make, or the reality that small changes over time can create meaningful new value.) We look at incremental and exponential as a spectrum. That said, we declare our bias for the exponential. And we think you should consider it too.*

Legacy media is a perfect example.

Just look at the entire landscape of Tier 2 business publications.

Is *Inc* better than *Forbes*? Is *Forbes* better than *Fortune*? Is *Fortune* better than *Business Insider*? Is *Business Insider* better than *FastCompany*?

The net of it is: nobody cares.

They're all in a race to the bottom.

When companies compete on features, price, and "brand," they drive down margins collectively, which limits growth—and the value of the category plummets.

All of this happens for two reasons:

1. Business people have been enrolled in the cult of Product.

"The best product wins."

Oh, really?

Domino's Pizza is a terrible product. But can you name a single next-best delivery pizza alternative?

Lululemon is a mediocre product (with a misogynist founder). But can you name another meaningful athleisure apparel company?

Products don't speak for themselves (regardless of how often this belief gets Tweeted around Silicon Valley). Products exist within the context of the category. Our favorite example here is the wheel—arguably the most impactful "product" on planet earth. Well, it took 300 years to turn the thing on its side and start using the product for transportation instead of pottery. How come the wheel couldn't speak for itself?

The category makes the product—not the other way around.

2. Business people have been enrolled in the cult of Brand.

"The best brand wins."

Oh, really?

Google has one of the most recognizable brands in the world. How come Google+ didn't work?

Microsoft has one of the most recognizable brands in the world. How come Microsoft stores failed so miserably?

Branding is important, but it is not the number one priority. The example we love to use here is the question, "Do you want to go to Tommy's for dinner?" Now, Tommy's could have the *best* brand in the whole wide world, but that's irrelevant until you have a more pressing question answered: "What kind of food do they have?" Before you can even consider whether or not you want Tommy's (brand), you need to know **what it is** (category). "Oh, Tommy's is authentic Italian food." Even still, the brand is irrelevant. You reply, "No thanks, I'm in the mood for sushi." (Different category.) And it's not until you decide on the category that you even become concerned with the brand.

So, why did Google+ fail? Why did Microsoft stores fail to "out-better" Apple?

Because the category makes the brand—not the other way around.

This also happens with entrepreneurs who believe THEY are "better" than other entrepreneurs.

Similar to companies that believe a "better product" strategy is the key to business success, many entrepreneurs start to drink their own Kool-aid once they gain a bit of traction. They believe it was their product, or their community, or the "movement" they created that was the reason for their success—not realizing each of those crucial components (product, community, business model, etc.) all live within the context of the category.

It's like gravity. You might not be conscious of its existence, but it's still there.

What really happened was they were *accidental category designers* the first time around. They stumbled into the right languaging, framed the problem, Named & Claimed the solution, and took the world by storm. However, because they weren't conscious of how or why things happened the way they did, they struggled to replicate their success a second time.

(*Which is why we encourage EVERYONE to become a category designer and pirate.* ***Arrrrrrrr!***)

This is the story of Andy Rubin, arguably one of the most legendary *accidental* category designers in technology history.

Andy created the Android operating system.

Unfortunately, as some engineers do, he thought it was the technology that made Android successful—and that was certainly a giant part of it. But more importantly, with the technology Andy also created a new category, which he Named & Claimed as an "open-source operating system for smartphones." (Legendary category names are often very descriptive.)

Clueless to his own category design, Andy eventually left to create his own smartphone company called Essential Phone ("essential" being a slightly more creative way of saying "better"). And investors (who just as often fall into the "better" trap) valued Andy's startup at over $1 billion before a single phone had even been shipped.

3 years later, the company folded.

Its phone, along with other highly anticipated "better-than" products, never materialized. Investors lost all their money.

It has been said that you will either be humble *in* life, or humbled *by* it. Well, the same way established brands think they can win in someone else's category based on their historical name and reputation, entrepreneurs can make the same exact mistake.

Because the category makes the entrepreneur—not the other way around.

Whenever we point out the "better" trap, the most common thing we hear back is, "I get it, but this sounds risky."

Let's talk about risk.

What's riskier? Competing in a $0 billion market you're trying to create, but doing so successfully means setting yourself up to earn 76% of the total value created?

Or, competing in a $1 billion market or a $10 billion market with a "better" strategy, which by definition means, *at most, **even if you win it ALL,*** the share you can expect is 24%?

If you are truly risk averse, the less risky strategy is to be a category designer and create *that which does not yet exist.* However, a large part of this is rooted in self-awareness, and being brutally honest about who you are and your intentions in business (do you want a legendary career or not?). Are you a mercenary, trying to take what you feel is yours, run out the clock, and hope you're not the last one out the door? Or are you a missionary, passionate about changing the world in some meaningful way (big or small), and willing to go on that journey regardless of whether or not people understand or accept you right away, give you validation and approval, or promise you a comfortable salary with a modest retirement account?

Oftentimes, people say they want to be the latter.

They say they want to live a life of purpose.

In reality, they're just trying to be "better" than the next guy or gal.

And they end up spending their whole lives fighting for one

tiny sliver from the remaining 24% of the pie as a result.

4

How To Dam The Demand

Most businesses fight for demand.

There is no finer example than the $80 billion-dollar industry dedicated to Search Engine Optimization. Here, companies and solopreneurs compete for the same handful of keywords and search terms, hoping to convince customers to click and purchase from them instead of one of their competitors. This is akin to kids jumping up and down yelling, "Pick me! Pick me!" Or muscle men walking around on stage in front of judges with numbers on their teeny-tiny mankinis, hoping they'll get picked for the trophy.

From early in life, we're taught to compete in a pre-existing game of comparison designed by someone else (read this sentence 3 times).

In doing so, we unconsciously submit to someone else's rules.

In business, this seems smart. Buy Google Ads for the keywords that indicate someone is already shopping and yell, "Pick me! Pick me!" The unquestioned rationale is: demand exists, and if our business can tap into that existing demand, we will find customers—and customers lead to profits.

There's just one problem.

Businesses that compete for demand fall into product comparison conversations—often in categories with existing leaders.

They walk into these existing markets saying, "We do the thing the already established Category Queen does, just better/faster/smarter/stronger/cheaper." The founders, investors, and well-educated executives who champion this business strategy believe they are doing the smart thing, de-risking their efforts by bringing an improvement to a proven market.

These people are not Pirates.

Here's why:

In order to become a Fortune 100 fastest-growing company, you have to have $50M in revenue and $10M in net income for the prior four quarters. You must also have grown revenues 20% per year for the previous three years. Through our research, we have found that 21% of the 600 or so companies that have held spots on the Fortune 100 fastest-growing list are, without question, category creators.

For 79% of fast-growing companies, $1.00 of revenue growth = $1.77 in market cap growth.

But compare that to the 21% that are category creators, and

$1.00 of revenue growth = $4.82 of market cap growth—nearly 3x higher.

When you are the creator and designer of the category, you are Queen/King—and the industry or market you create becomes your kingdom. You write the rules. You define its measures for success. And most importantly, you benefit the most from the category's growth.

You "win."

So, how do you capitalize on existing demand without falling into the product-comparison race to the bottom?

You Dam The Demand.

Often when we introduce newcomers to the concept of category design, the response we hear is, "How do we create something out of nothing? Creating demand out of thin air sounds hard and risky."

You're right.

Which is why a "DAM the demand" strategy is so powerful. It's about interrupting customers when they are shopping, and then educating them on the advantages of heading in a new and different direction. ("You think you *want that*, but you really *need this!*)

This is the Aikido (Japanese martial arts) move of category design, using the momentum of the legacy category to your advantage. When you successfully Dam The Demand, you raise an urgent question in the customer's mind:

"I thought I wanted X, but maybe what I really need is Y?"

And it's in this question—this gap between *what they thought they wanted* and *what they didn't know they needed*—where you have the opportunity to educate customers on the differences between the old category and the new one you are creating/designing. Dam The Demand is not a product-to-product comparison. It is a category vs category debate, and involves telling the truth about the legacy category and using the enemy's strengths (acknowledged by them and everyone in the category) *against* them.

There is no sales pitch, no shouting match, no "Pick me! Pick me!"

Just a cool, calm, and collected education on "The Gap" between what the market considers to be the best (or sometimes, the only) solution, and what they should now consider as a new and different way forward. And it's this truth-telling that stops customers in their tracks—because beholden as they might be to the legacy category, they are also painfully aware of its limitations. Further, this truth-telling permanently disables the existing Category Queen and all the competitors chasing "existing demand" in the old category.

Because when you Dam The Demand, you're moving buyers in the category FROM the old TO the new.

Here's how you Dam The Demand:

Step 1: Tell the truth about the existing category by placing a differentiating word in front.

It's not a car. It's an electric car.
  It's not a watch. It's a smart watch.
  It's not a computer. It's a personal computer.
  It's not a book. It's an eBook.
  It's not software. It's cloud software.
  It's not a desk. It's a treadmill desk.

The modification tells customers "this is different" while piquing their interest in the new, re-designed version of the existing category. "New" is a powerful word. It triggers the human mind to perk up and pay attention—meeting them where they are, interrupting their thought process, and then grabbing them by the hand and walking them in a different direction. **This framework becomes even more powerful when the modifier hints at one of the most commonly accepted pain points of the legacy category.** For example, in the old world of books, pages are made of paper. They're heavy. You can only carry so many physical books in your backpack. It's a problem for readers on-the-go. The modification "e" (implying digital) tells customers, "The problem you are used to experiencing in the legacy category no longer exists in this new and different future."

Second, notice how the modifier hints at the pain point without beating the customer over the head. It raises questions that spark the curiosity of the customer to learn more. It *shows* versus *tells*. In politics, it's the difference between an issue advertisement (which attempts to educate the public about something they aren't aware of) versus a negative advertisement (which attempts to denigrate the competition). The latter isn't what ultimately makes the difference. And when done correctly, truth-telling gets the customer to forget competition ever existed in the first place.

Third, notice how this modifier word is not an attempted amplification within the existing category—which is the mistake most companies make. "It's not just a watch, it's the *best* watch," a business might say, hoping the word "best" acts as a megaphone for their undifferentiated marketing. Unfortunately, this languaging mistake ends up having the inverse effect, prompting customers to ask, "Best *in relation to what?*"

And all of a sudden, you're in a product comparison conversation again.

Finally, notice how much more difficult it would be to get a book customer's attention if you said, "You should buy this new Wabloo!" The customer has no idea what a Wabloo is (and neither do we)—and because it requires an additional sentence (or five) of explanation in order to help them understand, the customer has already made the subconscious decision they don't care. They've moved on. Furthermore, because you are attempting to invent a new word instead of modifying an existing word, you are forgoing the opportunity to tap into any existing demand that exists in the legacy category.

Other times, new categories are named by what they're not.

Henry Ford called the first car a "horseless carriage."

He used a modifier to remove the existing category's most valuable asset (there is no horse), raising the question, "Well if there's no horse, then how does it run?"

Ah, now the customer is willing to be educated!

They have entered "The Gap," and are open to being moved *from* the existing category *to* the new and different category they didn't know they needed.

Step 2: Fine-tune the modifier so that it doesn't highlight just an issue with the product, but an issue with the fundamental business model of the legacy category.

Let's use Netflix as an example.

Binge-watching is so common now, it requires us to go back and remember how we used to watch TV. It used to be, "appointment TV," where TV executives deemed it a success when the viewers would revolve their schedules and lives around show times.

When Netflix released House of Cards in 2013, it dropped the entire season all at once. Wall Street was convinced this was the stupidest decision ever, since consumers could sign up, binge-watch, then cancel their subscription. We disagreed. In a piece for Harvard Business Review, we called it a radically generous strategy that consumers would understand and reciprocate. Netflix said fewer than 8,000 people signed up, binged and canceled—or 0.6% of the 1.3 million people who signed up for a trial in January of 2013.

"Windowing," the opposite of binge-watching, was the word for the legacy network TV business and how they released new episodes. The business model works like this: pick a bunch of pilots, shoot a few episodes, and drop them a week at a time. For pilots that attract viewers, the network invests in filming the rest of the season. For pilots that don't immediately hook audiences, the TV network cuts their losses and scraps the series. The result here is an industry-wide obsession over TV ratings, which are based upon audience demographics watching a given show. The more people within a certain demographic watching a show, the higher the rating. And the higher the rating, the more the TV network can charge for their advertising inventory.

Since the underlying business model for network TV is advertising, these companies don't have the luxury of giving all twelve episodes of a show to the viewer at once. It goes against their "test then invest" production strategy, and more importantly, shortens the amount of time they can put ads in front of the viewer. It's an incredibly risk-averse business model, and one where the show runner and creator is just a cog in the machine.

With "binge-watching," Netflix puts the viewer at the center of their business model—driving a stake through the heart of the legacy category's business model.

They *want* the viewer to binge as much as they want. Because the more content viewers can binge, the stickier they are to their subscription. As a result, Netflix (and in their footsteps, other streaming platforms) is incentivized to produce entire seasons and give all the episodes away at once. This is incredibly attractive to show runners who want the creative freedom to tell their stories across entire seasons, not a pilot plus a few episodes.

"Binge-watching" didn't just DAM the demand. It put a massive wrench in the legacy category's business model.

When this is done successfully, the Queen of the new and different category places the legacy category into check on the chessboard. Now, it's only a matter of time—and the unraveling of the old world begins to accelerate. You know this is working when an uprising happens on both sides of the chessboard: the incumbents start shouting about how "crazy" this new and different reality sounds, while the new Category Queen and all her evangelists chant louder and louder about the benefits that come with this new and different future.

There are infinite examples of this—our current favorite being the war between the legacy business media category (*New York Times*) and the new Direct-To-Creator media category (Substack). The old world says, "That's not real journalism!" Meanwhile, the new category just keeps speaking the truth: "Hey writers: if you write the content but they make all the money, isn't that sort of like being held hostage?"

Step 3: Once you Dam The Demand, you are free to educate customers on the differences between the old category and this new and different category.

Dam it, then expand it.

The way you do this is by tapping into your Superconsumers. Think of your Supers as the traffic conductors standing at the bridge from the old to the new. They're the ones wearing bright green neon vests waving their arms in the air telling everyone they know about the benefits of going right instead of left. These Supers are the ones who adopt your different POV and then evangelize your new category point of view using the language you gave them. They are literally saying the old category's name with the new modifier.

This is word-of-mouth marketing at its finest.

Word of mouth is and always will be the most powerful form of marketing. Category designers make sure the right words come out of the right (Supers') mouths, changing the narrative and moving the world as a result.

When this happens, exponential growth is unlocked—and in many cases, the TAM for the new category ends up being much bigger than the TAM of the legacy category. And as the category "tips" (a term coined by legendary author, Malcolm Gladwell, in his book *The Tipping Point*), customers pull the product out of the category winner. They *have to have it*.

Ever seen people camping overnight in front of an Apple store to get the new iPhone?

The Story of Peloton

Now, let's see these 3 steps in action.

Here's how Peloton successfully executed a Dam The Demand strategy. ***Arrrrrrrr!***

In the '90s and 2000s, "indoor cycling classes" were all the rage. This new category of workout class was created by Mad Dogg Athletics—and they did such a legendary category design job that the brand "Spinning" became the category name, much like how "Band-Aid" morphed from the brand name to the category name. This is category design at its finest.

Well, for a long time, Spinning looked unbeatable—until Peloton started to Dam The Demand. In 2012, Peloton's founder John Foley set out to build a company with a radically different point of view. "Why go to a Spinning class when the class can come to you?" This POV was so different, Foley estimates he was rejected upwards of 5,000 times from investors.

Step 1: Modify the existing category

Foley created a Dam The Demand opportunity by placing a modifier in front of the existing category.

Home Fitness.

Peloton wasn't a "better" workout. It was a Home Workout. And it wasn't a "better" spin class. It was a Home or Virtual spin class. No product-to-product comparisons, no feature-to-feature discussions.

As a result, customers started asking themselves, "Hang on a second. I can have a cycling class in my living room? How would that even work?"

Peloton makes their DAM the demand strategy very clear on their website:

> *"In 2012, we brought the best talent in technology, hardware and production together to accomplish an ambitious goal: bring the community and excitement of boutique fitness into the home. In order to design a new category of "home fitness."*

Step 2: Fine-tune the modifier so that it doesn't highlight just an issue with the product, but an issue with the fundamental business model of the legacy category.

Words matter.

The words "Home Workout" or "Virtual Spin Class" imply all the problems with the existing category. "My regular spin class is across town. It takes me 40 minutes to get there. I can never find a place to park. I get charged even if I can't attend. If I'm late, they won't let me in."

And so on, and so on.

This is what customers start to realize: they're getting screwed. And now that they've been educated, now that they see a reality where they can take a spin class from home, there's no going back. In 2015, Bloomberg published a piece titled, *The Most Exclusive Spin Class Is In Your Living Room* (referring to Peloton as Virtual Spinning).

Step 3: Once you Dam The Demand, educate customers on all the differences between the old category and this new and different category.

Again, you know it's working when there is an uprising on both sides of the chessboard.

From 2014 to when Peloton went public in 2019, the fitness industry was up in arms over the idea of working out from home. "It's a fad. It's a trend." The incumbents found Peloton's point of view and new category to be ridiculous.

But the war was already over—the rest of the fitness industry just didn't know it yet.

Over time, Peloton didn't just Dam The Demand for the legacy mega-category, but expanded into other subcategories and niches as well. They now sell "Home Fitness" everything: home fitness treadmills, home fitness boxing, accessories, apparel, and more (remember: new categories create more new categories).

Peloton won.

The result, of course, is Sophie's Choice: each answer is painful. The legacy category leader has been jammed into a corner they can't fight their way out of. If Spinning stays put, they will live in an ever-shrinking category and remain Queen of Irrelevant Island. And if they jump into the new Home Fitness category, like they have, they become Pepsi—forever in Coke's shadow.

This is the knockout punch.

Spinning is screwed, no matter how much "better" they make the product.

You never want to be in a product-to-product competition.

What you want to do instead is change the definition of what the category is (by placing a modifier in front of it), giving you the opportunity to rewrite the rules.

The example we love to use is the dynamic that gets set when a company issues an RFP (Request For Proposal).

An RFP is essentially a document stating the rules of the game: "We are a fintech startup seeking a branding and marketing agency to help us redesign our website and marketing materials." In this scenario, agencies take the instructions from the RFP and *compete* for the job. (Just like the muscle men in their mankinis.) One agency will tout their ability to get branding and marketing projects done on schedule. Another will highlight their specific branding and marketing knowledge of the fintech industry. Another will emphasize their cost-effective branding and marketing solutions. And so on.

But what the participating agencies fail to realize is that they are all, simultaneously, having a comparison discussion. "Who we are, *compared to other branding and marketing agencies*, is better/faster/smarter/stronger/cheaper."

However, when you Dam The Demand, you take the RFP of the category, rewrite it, and then educate the person who originally handed you the RFP document on why they're following the legacy treasure map—and why your new & different treasure map is the one that leads to the treasure *they didn't know they wanted.*

"You see, we're not a branding and marketing agency," you might say. "We're Category Design consultants —which is different from branding and marketing agencies. But that doesn't sound like what you're interested in." *Your voice trails off, as if about to hang up the phone.*

"Well hang on, before I let you go," the decision-maker on the other end of the line says, "I'm curious. Then what is a Category Design Consultant?"

[You have now entered "The Gap"]

"Oh, as Category Design experts we specialize in helping companies like yours come up with the strategy and language that educates customers on why you are new and different. When you do this successfully, you have no competitors. You stand alone. But again, it sounds like you have your mind made up about wanting to hire a conventional branding and marketing agency to better compete in an existing market," you say, *again letting your voice trail off, as if about to hang up the phone.*

"Well hang on, what you're saying is exactly what we've been talking about in our board meetings. We want to be seen as the leader in our category, and so that's why we thought of doing a re-brand." (Most of the time, the people issuing RFPs don't even know why they're asking for what they're asking for. Further, most re-brands are about competing—and a "brand strategy" in the absence of a category strategy often devolves into an asinine exercise about colors, logos, and meaningless taglines.)

[Meanwhile, somewhere in New York, an entire floor of mediocrely paid copywriters and designers are hard at work on a very fancy, competition-minded response to the RFP.]

When you are responding to an RFP, you've already lost. Or, as we wrote about in our previous letter on career design, if you are responding to a job posting, you are a candidate playing a comparison game ("I'm smarter than you. My alma mater is better known than yours. I've been doing this longer than you have.") And yet, companies respond to the RFP written by the existing demand in the market all the time. They think their customer wants branding and marketing services, and so they shout, "WE HAVE AMAZING BRANDING AND MARKETING SERVICES." (Aka "Pick me! Pick me!") They think their customer wants a digital camera, and so they shout, "WE HAVE THE CHEAPEST DIGITAL CAMERAS." They think their customer wants a used car, and so they shout, "WE HAVE THE BEST USED CARS OF ANY DEALERSHIP IN THE LOCAL AREA."

They are doing their darndest to respond to the RFP of the industry—when they should be doing their damnedest to Dam The Demand, stop customers in their tracks, engage in business Aikido, and redirect the momentum of the category in the direction of their choosing.

When you help the company or customer rewrite the RFP, suddenly you are the one determining the rules of the game.

And guess who wins when the rules get re-designed?
You.
The category designer.

5

The Lightning Strike Strategy

Most annual marketing planning is an orgy of frustration and mental masturbation.

(An image of a conference room—or, in today's digital world, a bunch of Zoom boxes muting and unmuting—of executives tripping over each other, spurting out "creative ideas" and a long list of "P1 priorities" should come to mind.)

At best, a company will audit its metrics from the previous year and decide which initiatives to spend more money incrementally improving. At its worst, the CFO is the one coming up with the slogan that's going to go on the billboards the company is planning to run for their next product launch. Either way, annual marketing planning is usually about as fun and productive as getting hit with a hockey puck in the privates.

The first problem with marketing plans is most of them start with last year's marketing plan as the template.

But legendary plans are about creating a different future. Not continuing the past.

And as your shipmates, we are here to help you right the ship.

The 3 Pillars Of Every Great Marketing Strategy: Information Wars, Air Wars, and Ground Wars

To begin, it's important we outline what a legendary marketing strategy looks like.

Every startup, company, and creator is fighting 3 different types of wars at the same time: the war for who frames the problem, names and claims the solution, and as a result owns the narrative (The Information Wars); the war for who is then able to most effectively "sell" that narrative at scale (The Air Wars); and the war for who can best convert new recruits to the war effort—prospect to prospect, customer to customer, consumer to consumer, and thus make the cash register sing (The Ground Wars).

Here's a quick summary of each:

Information Wars: This is what sets the strategic context. (Context is everything.) It's the combination of ways in which you educate the world about the category you're designing, AND, learning from your Superconsumers (and amplifying their voices) to accelerate your effectiveness both in the air and on the ground. (This is more focused on POV marketing / word of mouth than anything else.)

Air Wars: In many ways, marketing is "sales at scale." Air Wars are the high-level strategic marketing initiatives you do in service of the new and different category you are creating in the world, all the while positioning yourself as the leader. These efforts are more focused on demand *creation*.

Ground Wars: This is tactical marketing (often at the point-of-sale and heavily integrated with sales) that supports your strategic efforts marketing the category and driving near-term revenue. (*Ca-Ching, Ca-Ching.*) These efforts are more focused on demand *capture* and lead generation.

Now, let's walk through what this looks like in action.

The Story of Malibu Mylk

Every once in a while, we Pirates hop aboard another pirate ship to lend a helping hand.

Malibu Mylk is a startup we have been working with to help create a new sub-category called "whole-plant organic flax milk." Within the mega-category of "alternative milk" (basically anything that qualifies as milk but isn't dairy), there is a sub-category with a strong tailwind called "plant-based milk." However, not everyone jives with plant-based milk. Some people can't drink certain types of alternative milks because they have a soy allergy, or a nut allergy. This was Brittany's story, the founder of Malibu Mylk. When Brittany Fuisz was dealing with some health issues, she went to see a functional medicine doctor who told her she needed to eliminate dairy, nuts, gluten, and soy from her diet.

The problem was, every "milk alternative" in the market had some sort of allergen. Soy milk is made from soybeans. Almond milk is made from nuts. Oat milk is made from grains (the vast majority of which contain some form of gluten). For someone going 100% allergen free, there were no "alternative milk" options.

So, Brittany created one—out of flax.

The Information War: Educating customers on the benefits of whole-plant organic flax.

The first war Malibu Mylk has to fight is educating people on why they should consider flax milk as a viable "milk alternative."

Remember, The Information War is all about three things: your unique POV (what are you saying?), your Languaging (how are you saying it?), and your Superconsumers (who do you want repeating what you're saying?). In Malibu Mylk's case, this meant helping design new language to talk about this new type of product.

Some of what we came up with:

- **"Whole-plant" as distinct from "plant-based."** Many foods that aren't actually healthy for you (and are filled with other unhealthy ingredients) can call themselves "plant-based," so using old language to describe a new & different thing would be a mistake. Too many "plant-based milks" strain out the majority of the plant and then add in a lot of non-plant baddies (like rapeseed oil) that many would be surprised to find out about. Actually, most "plant-based milks" are kind of like how some movies "based on real events" end up being marginally based on the truth.
- **100% allergen free.** Flax, in and of itself, isn't what the customer cares about. What makes flax interesting is that, in the context of (mega-category) "alternative milks" and (sub-category) "plant-based milks," flax milk is the only one that is 100% allergen free. This is the *position* the product then owns in the customers mind.
- **The benefits of flax.** Once the customer understands that

position, it's also great to tell them flax is the largest source of vegan omega-3s, aids in digestion, is anti-inflammatory, and also sustainable for the environment (whereas it takes over 20 gallons of water to produce a single glass of almond milk).

The Information War for Malibu Mylk is all about (in this order) getting this POV, and these words, into the mouths of Superconsumers of health, wellness, and "alternative milks."

But wait, there's more!

Pirate Eddie then discovered something interesting. Within the niche of health, wellness, and "alt milk" Superconsumers is actually an *even more specific, more potent* niche of more relevant Supers for this particular product. (We can't tell you who though because that's the *secret sauce* that's worth $5 million bucks.)

These Superconsumers are not just of "health" in general, but their health in a more specific context. Which just so happens to be Brittany's story as well. (This is a great example of Founder/Category alignment—the right person, solving the right problem, with a highly relevant personal story and perspective.) This is the level of nuance you should be thinking about within your own marketing. And why it's so crucial to have clarity around your unique POV (Pirate Christopher's specialty), new words that communicate your different POV (Pirate Cole's specialty), and a data-driven understanding of who your Superconsumers are (Pirate Eddie's specialty).

See why they call us the Category Pirates?

The Air Wars for Malibu Mylk are then all about getting relevant media, influencers, and of course their Superconsumers to talk about this different POV *at scale*—and for the company to publish content and launch campaigns that educate other Supers on this different POV at scale.

The Ground Wars for Malibu Mylk mean Brittany interacting with relevant Superconsumers herself, or empowering her sales team to interact with and educate Supers directly. For example, something Brittany does when she goes to the grocery store is she walks around and looks for women who put almond, oat, or soy milk in their carts, stops them, introduces herself, and offers them the opportunity to give flax milk a try. This is hand-to-hand "combat", and ground war marketing at its finest. This is a Dam The Demand strategy IRL ("in real life," for all our Boomer Pirates out there). Malibu Mylk then does the same thing in the digital world at the point of purchase. When someone searches for Oat Milk online, they are likely to see an ad for Malibu Mylk's flax milk.

The key is to align all three.

The mix matters.

When a company over-rotates and disproportionately spends more marketing dollars and people hours in any one of these areas, they usually run into a problem. Either they spend too much time and money or both trying to "sell at scale" (Air Wars), not realizing they don't have boots on the ground (Ground Wars) to effectively convert those prospects into customers. Or they become too myopic and focused on winning each individual battle (Ground Wars) that they forget what cause they're fighting for in the first place (Information War).

Where marketing planning goes wrong:

Unfortunately, some companies are extremely myopic.

All they do is ground wars.

Pirate Christopher was once in a meeting with a public tech company CEO who said, "We make shit, we sell shit, and everything else is bullshit."

For these companies, there is very little discussion around The Information War. Agenda item, "Debate the premise," doesn't exist. Everyone in the room just sort of accepts the premise, accepts that the POV for the company *is fine, has always been fine, and will go on being fine,* and all they need to do is figure out whether to spend more money on Facebook ads or Instagram ads and come up with a tagline for the new product being launched in March.

This is what makes marketing planning so "fun" (aka: horribly unproductive).

Everyone thinks they are a marketing expert.

People with no training or experience in finance rarely render their opinion about how to do accounting. People with no training or experience in product development rarely render their opinion about how to make products. But people with no training or experience in marketing almost always express their opinion about how to do marketing. We've been in more meetings than we can remember where non-marketing executives fought vigorously for their "idea." (We once knew a CTO who wanted the company's new enterprise software category to be called a "Thing Tracker.")

When you are a CMO, you are constantly being given a lot of "help."

And the reason marketing leaders get so much "help" is because everyone experiences marketing all day, every day. So in their minds, they *are* experts—because they are consumers of marketing. (We know what great food tastes like, but we don't think that makes us great chefs.)

People tend to treat marketing just like any other form of content. They apply the same lens to marketing that they apply to a movie, a book, or naming their cat: "Do I like it?" For example, we were once in a meeting where a CMO was proposing a new color pallet for the company brand, which included orange. The second the CEO saw the new colors, he grizzled, "ORANGE!? Don't you know that ORANGE makes people angry!?" We were not (and still are not) aware of any data science that shows this, but we sure know orange makes one guy angry!

The "do I like it" lens is for fools. Yet, it is the lens most used when evaluating marketing. But the right lens is, "Does this work?" And by "work" we mean, "Does this marketing help us design and dominate a giant category that matters?" That's the lens to evaluate marketing plans, campaigns, and executions—and just like a great CFO in respect to accounting, very few people are trained, experienced, and qualified to effectively answer that question for an organization.

So, when looking at a new marketing plan, do NOT look at the idea through the "Do I like this?" lens.

Look at it through the "Does this work?" lens.

As a founder, CEO, or CMO, we encourage you to use all of this as context at the start of any marketing planning session.

Unfortunately, most founders, CEOs, and CMOs will ignore this advice entirely. And will go on debating whether or not the company should make a TikTok page.

However, if you hear what we're saying and are thinking, "You know what? These guys might be onto something," then we encourage you to invest a third of your resources and budget into each area of marketing: winning The Information War, Air Wars, and Ground Wars. Test and tweak over the quarters. And also understand that it takes 6-10 years to create a category and have it tip at scale. So if the whole world doesn't immediately understand the value of your new and different product, service, or idea in the first 30 days, don't get discouraged. (Sun Microsystems became the server platform Category Queen back in the dot-com era by proclaiming, "The Network Is The Computer." It took a while for people to "get" their POV. But when they did, people understood the genius of it.)

Until then, you can still drive sales and generate revenue NOW by meeting customers where they currently are and using a Dam The Demand strategy.

When targeted at your Supers with the right Languaging, you can start creating revenue fast.

So, to recap:

- **The Information War:** What you're saying (POV), how (Languaging), to whom (your Superconsumers).
- **The Air Wars:** How you are taking your unique and differentiated POV & Languaging and educating your Superconsumers at scale.
- **The Ground Wars:** How you are empowering yourself, your team, and your Superconsumers to educate and enlist other potential Superconsumers to BUY NOW and become loyal supporters of your new and different category over time.

This is your marketing strategy. Always and forever.

All that said, sequencing matters.

So let's break down each one.

1. Information Wars

Jim Morrison famously said, "Control the media, control the mind." And Victor Hugo said, "An invasion of armies can be resisted; an invasion of ideas cannot."

As we've said, The Information War is all about putting the right words (Languaging) in the right mouths (Superconsumers), empowering your Supers to run from town to town and tell everyone, "They won! They won!"

The same way disinformation can spread like wildfire (especially in today's digital world), "information marketing" can spread just as fast. For example, a few years ago, legendary copywriter Craig Clemens came up with an information marketing campaign that changed the world. He called it,

"The American Parasite," and wrote a 30+ minute sales letter educating the general public about a problem they did not know they had: "leaky gut."

And who grabbed onto it?

All the biggest health nuts—ranging from medical doctors to Oprah.

As a result, this POV put the right words ("leaky gut") in the right mouths (food, diet, and nutrition Superconsumers), who went out into the world to educate as many people as they could about the importance of proactively defending against "leaky gut" by taking *probiotics*. (New category... at least for the general public.)

That information war POV ended up selling more than $100 million worth of probiotics *in its first year*, and to date, Craig's business, Golden Hippo (which owns and operates a portfolio of health and wellness brands) is one of the largest sellers of probiotics in the country.

Another example:

Pirate Cole and his co-captain, Pirate Dickie deployed a similar Information War strategy with their cohort-based writing community, Ship 30 for 30.

Ship 30 for 30 is a cohort-based writing challenge & curriculum where writers are challenged to write 30 "Atomic Essays" in 30 days. So, how do you get an idea like that to spread? Well, when a customer hops aboard, they are able to unlock an archive of previous videos and exclusive live sessions from prior cohorts by sharing a message on Twitter. This first step creates a flywheel where every new signup then tells their own audience about their involvement in the program.

Then, once the cohort begins, the flywheel spins faster and faster because each "Shipper" is challenged to write and publish 30 Atomic Essays in 30 days. Where do they write these essays? On Typeshare, a software product built and owned by the Ship 30 team. And where do they publish these essays? On Twitter—where each "Shipper" is then educating their own audiences on a) what Ship 30 for 30 is, b) what it looks like to be involved, and c) what results prospects can expect (since they are watching their friends achieve those results in public).

As a result, you can't interact with anyone on Twitter even one degree of separation away from Ship 30 for 30 without being inundated with little ship emojis and Atomic Essays flooding your feed.

Winning The Information War is about both having a differentiated POV (combined with differentiated Languaging) AND finding a way to get that POV and new Languaging in the mouths of Superconsumers. Do this, and it will be very hard for anyone to enter your new category without someone immediately tapping them on the shoulder and saying, "Oh! You mean like them, over there? They're the Category Leader. *Everyone* knows that."

2. Air Wars

Once you have your POV and Languaging locked and loaded, and are clear about exactly who your Superconsumers are (the people most open to something new and different, and most likely to go tell other people about that new and different), it's time to "sell at scale."

All of this starts with understanding: what's the war you are fighting, and why does it matter? (Not to you, but to the customer.)

Entrepreneurs, executives, investors, and marketers often forget that the context of the war is more important than the war itself. Why does anyone care who wins a fight? Because of what's at stake. Because of what winning and losing means. Two men beating on each other in a ring doesn't mean anything. But when you have the context that one of those men gave up his leadership position in boxing to take a stand against the Vietnam War, cost him millions of dollars, and was sent to prison, only to return to the ring once again years later, well, suddenly the context of the fight changes.

> *"In March 1966, after Muhammid Ali's draft status was reclassified and he became eligible to serve in the military, the champ made headlines around the world when he refused his induction into the U.S. armed forces, invoking his constitutional right to decline service as a conscientious objector. The Vietnam War was still supported by a majority of Americans at the time; Ali's decision to speak out against it was hugely controversial, and he was pilloried by politicians and the media as a coward and traitor. 'I ain't got nothing against them Vietcong,' explained Ali of his motivations. 'How can I shoot those poor people? Just take me to jail.' Ali was acting not from fear but from the strength of his convictions, and he paid a heavy price. In March 1967, he was stripped of his heavyweight title, and that June he was convicted of draft evasion and sentenced to five years in prison. He was effectively banned from boxing for three and a half years, stripped of his passport and unable to obtain a license to*

> *box in any state. Sacrificing the prime years of his career cost him untold millions, leaving him in debt and leading him years later to fight well past the point when he should have retired, absorbing damaging blows that many believe led to the Parkinson's disease he suffered from for the final three decades of his life."* – Rolling Stone

Context is everything.

Without a "why," no one cares about the "when," "where," "what," or "who."

When it comes to marketing your company, your products and services, or even yourself as an entrepreneur and/or creator, do not get it confused: your Air War efforts are not about you. They are about your raison d'être, your reason for waking up every day and pounding the pavement, and the cause you believe is more important than yourself.

For example:

- **Airbnb doesn't promote "Airbnb" (brand).** They promote "live like a local"" (category). And their rally cry, their reason for waking up every morning, is to help more people "live like a local," and experience the freedoms that get unlocked as a result of home-sharing. That's the POV they are trying to "sell at scale."
- **Salesforce doesn't promote "Salesforce" (brand).** They promote "the cloud" (category). Data in the cloud. Analytics in the cloud. Software management in the cloud. Customer service in the cloud. And now collaboration in the cloud (Slack). Everything the company does is in service of the larger war, which is dependent upon

businesses moving out of the old, legacy "on-premise" world, and entering the new "only software" world in the cloud.
- **Tesla doesn't promote "Tesla" (brand).** They promote "electric vehicles" and, more broadly, "sustainable energy" (category). Everything they do, and everything Elon Musk does, is *not* about ramming Tesla's brand down people's throats (that's for smooth-brained brand marketers in Detroit). It's about educating the world on the benefits of electric cars opposed to ICE (internal combustion engine) vehicles. They are driving (pun intended) a massive FROM-TO.

Air War efforts should be about taking your POV and selling it at scale, 24 hours per day, 7 days per week, in a way that isn't dependent upon you having individual conversations with each and every one of your potential Superconsumers. (They should be able to hear about it or discover it somewhere else, from someone else.)

Air Wars can be everything from:

- Publishing a whitepaper on the future of your category (and revealing industry leading research before anyone else).
- Holding conferences, masterminds, and events that educate customers, prospects, and partners on the future of your industry.
- "Trend jacking" what's currently attracting attention and continuing to remain relevant by inserting yourself into public conversations.

- Participating in the podcast circuit not just in your chosen category, but the 9 other categories your Superconsumers are also Supers in. (The sole purpose of this is to "geek out" about the problem and generate awareness.)
- Mass market advertising—but only if done well and with the purpose of advocating a category problem and POV.
- One ad, run once, that dramatically changes the context and conversation.

Anheuser-Busch Super Bowl Air Wars

Anheuser-Busch (pre-acquisition by InBev) is a great example of how Air Wars (and "selling at scale") works.

For years, they would routinely buy as many as 10 Superbowl spots.

At the time, it appeared wasteful. But legacy Anheuser-Busch executives knew what they were doing. At least some of their ads were not *just* meant for consumers, but as "red meat" to the independent wholesalers. Alcohol manufacturers are not able to own distribution in most of the US due to legacy three-tier distribution laws tied back to prohibition. And while they were under no obligation to carry Anheuser-Busch products, Anheuser knew honey attracted more flies than vinegar. They often ran "Here's to Beer" commercials that weren't tied to any new products or a specific Call to Action, but served as a reminder that they were in the "making friends" category. More immediately, it got the blood flowing for their distributors who would then go out and "stack them high and watch them fly."

Finally, when people understand why the war you're fighting matters, they will gladly show up in droves and enlist themselves to be part of your army. (And when they fail to understand why it matters, they will do as Muhummad Ali did and go to great lengths to avoid being associated with your kind.)

Tesla does this terrifically with their Tesla AI Day, Autonomous Day, and Battery Day events, which are primarily held in service of attracting more Superconsumers (within those respective categories) interested in thinking about the future, solving difficult problems, and even working for the company. These events are all about calling to attention a core piece of the problem to solve (in the emerging category), showing Tesla's progress to date, and then attracting the best talent to help Tesla crack the code.

3. Ground Wars

If Air Wars are about "selling at scale," and solidifying your future leadership position in the category, then Ground Wars are all about making the cash register sing *today*.

These are the individual battles that make it known who is really winning in the trenches (and whose planes they should cheer for when they fly overhead). If you are a CMO, your number one job (as soon as you hop aboard) is to prove you know how to win some ground wars. If you are the CMO of a B2B company, this means filling the pipeline with leads. And if you are a CMO in the B2C space, this means doing practical, tactical, cost-effective marketing that makes a difference in revenue within the first 6 months.

Otherwise, you're gone.

Because if the company has a "growth problem," the CMO gets axed. And if that doesn't work, the CEO gets fired.

> *Also remember company growth must be looked at in the context of the category. You might hear that Company A is growing at 75% and think that sounds great. But if the category designer (Company B) is growing at 125%, Company A is likely on the road to zombie. Context matters.*

Ground Wars can be everything from:

- **Dam the demand marketing, where you intercept another category's point-of-sale and convert it to your own.** For example, Ball Park Hot Dogs executives, Steve Clapp and Carl Gerlach, figured out their Supercon-sumer (households with teen boys) and the key use case (after-school snack) carried a massively disproportionate amount of profit in the category. These teen boys were so ravenously hungry after school, they devoured anything easy to eat (chips, cookies, cereal, etc.). So Steve and Carl decided to Dam The Demand for carb snacks by marketing the POV "30 seconds to heat, 30 seconds to eat" to teen boys via video games and x-sports. It wasn't a hot dog. It was a protein rich quick meal. And in 5 years, they went from #2 to #1 and doubled revenue while keeping their marketing budget flat. Marc Benioff did the same thing in B2B tech, damming the demand by educating Supers: "You think you want 'on-premise' CRM, but what you really need is Cloud CRM."
- **Aggregating customer testimonials from their origin**

story: How these Supers became aware and entered the category, what triggered them to buy (the tipping point), and how the category changed their company, their career, and their lives as a result (outcome/transformation vignettes). It's even better if all these aggregated customer stories and testimonials are happening on emerging platforms, becoming evergreen assets that benefit from the growth of the new ecosystem. However, don't get it confused: the platform is not as important as the POV you are evangelizing, the Languaging you are giving your Superconsumers, and the stories you are telling and curating as a result. If the content is specific enough and valuable enough, people will go wherever they need to go in order to consume it (including reading physical mail).

- **Moving a thoughtful percentage of your advertising budget to emerging mediums, often closer to the point of sale.** Remember back in 2012 when people thought Facebook ads were expensive? For direct-to-consumer companies, this means advertising on Amazon and Google and optimizing SEO. For consumer packaged goods companies, this means smart merchandising, shelving, price/promotion and other retail advertising. And for B2B companies, winning often involves interrupting potential customers when they first start the investigation / consideration stage of the customer life cycle. Legacy category leaders have created demand that a prospect starts to investigate. It's then your job to enter with a POV to Dam The Demand.

- **Holding events for Superconsumers held in Supergeos,** where prospects and potential customers see hordes of Superconsumers gathering and geeking out about the

category—and get infected with demand as a result.
- **New product launch events,** especially when beta-versions are released to Superconsumers to try, test, tweak, and tell others to get it. There's no marketing like co-opting your Superconsumers as your very best sales and marketing folks.

However, where marketers, entrepreneurs, executives, and well-intentioned investors go wrong here is they put all their focus on the tactical and forget the strategic. They forget capturing existing demand, created by someone else, is one skill—and damming or creating demand, well, that is a very particular (and exponentially more valuable) set of skills.

Synchronizing Your Information, Air, and Ground War Strategies

When aligned, this is how you get 1 + 1 + 1 = 30 billion.

Your Air War efforts are what give your Ground War efforts clarity (employees, especially, need to know why their work matters and why they should dedicate years of their lives to your mission). Similarly, your Ground War efforts manufacture revenue. (You can't call yourself "the leader" if you aren't able to win any battles—aka produce any sales!). And if you can win the Information War, your Air War and Ground War efforts just got exponentially easier (assuming Superconsumers are speaking about your company in the way you intended.) Where The Information War gets lost is when Superconsumers start using their own language to describe who you are and what you do, positioning you into a corner you didn't necessarily intend.

You want your community to sing *your song*. Not make up thousands of songs on their own.

Said differently, the way you align and synchronize your efforts is by not over-spending in any one direction.

If you can win the Information War and build a legendary distribution flywheel where your Superconsumers do all the marketing for you, chances are, you don't need to spend as much money putting planes in the sky and boots on the ground. Similarly, if you are a Fortune 500 company with zero direct-to-customer distribution, you're probably better off investing in building your own bases than Super Bowl ads (Air War) that don't help prospects take immediate action.

When you deploy your resources is paramount to your success.

So, how do you get these three to align?

Why The Marketing Department Needs To Have A Direct Relationship With The Finance Department

Listen to the way most CMOs talk about their budget, and what you'll hear is this:

"I'm not sure that's in **my** budget."

Most CMOs at both large companies and rapidly scaling startups think of the marketing budget as "theirs." And what they got hired to do was to be the arbiter of what gets spent, where, based on their own individual wants and needs.

In reality, this sort of behavior is the reason CMOs are often told to sit at the kids table. They aren't treated as true executives, and oftentimes are left out of "adult conversations" between the CEO, COO, CPO and CFO or CRO. (It's not uncommon then for the acting CMO, when left out of a meeting regarding the strategy of the entire company, to clench his or her fists and stomp on the ground, insisting, "Hey! I'm an executive too!")

The truth is, as a CMO, the marketing budget isn't **your** budget.

It's the company's budget.

Just like the product budget isn't the Head of Engineering's budget, and the HR budget isn't the Head of HR's budget. Everyone works for the same company. Marketing just happens to be the largest discretionary budget in the company. And while other budgets—such as sales, product development, HR, etc.—are intimately tied to headcount, marketing is the only place where there doesn't have to be a correlation between the number of employees and the amount the company is willing to invest. In addition, marketing is the only place where the company can (on a whim) either cut back radically, or spray gasoline and crank up the furnace radically.

As a result, marketing becomes one big honeypot of money everyone is trying to stick their hand in. And many in the company will try their hardest to get a chunk of the marketing budget for themselves—leading to a death of 1,000 cuts.

- The product manager says, "I'm rolling out a new product in March."
- The sales manager says, "We need more leads in this territory."
- The product designer says, "We need beta testers."
- Etc.

This is not a very strategic or intelligent way of thinking about (or using) your marketing budget. It's the mistake that causes "marketing" to turn into a service bureau for "serving internal customers." We've even heard marketing people say stuff like, "Our goal is to add value to *the business*." As if marketing was some external appendage and not part of the business. Like there is *the real business* and then there are support functions of which "marketing" is one.

If your CEO and/or CMO think and talk like this, quit.

Become Best Friends With The CFO/CRO

If you want to run a legendary organization and do legendary marketing, you must have a legendary relationship with the finance department.

Savvy CMOs work directly with the CFO to create a strategic escape valve for the company every quarter. If you've been the CMO of a global company like Procter & Gamble for the past 10 years, this is probably something you are intimately familiar with (and if not, then hey ho, let's go). If you're the CFO, CEO, or CMO of a newly public company or startup about to IPO, you might have *heard* about this but have yet to figure out how to implement it into the organization. And if you are a newer company with newer entrepreneurs and executives, or are a first-time CMO yourself, then what we are about to tell you is probably going to be a bit like learning the earth isn't flat after all.

Since the marketing budget is the largest discretionary budget in the company, it should not be thought of as "the marketing budget." It should be thought of as "the company's budget," of which marketing has the most flexibility and creative potential.

However, in order to do anything of consequence with a company's marketing budget, it's crucial to understand how that budget sits in the context of the rest of the company—which is why the CMO needs to work directly with the CFO.

When there is a direct line of communication, the CFO may ask the CMO to take a percentage of the quarterly budget (often from the "Air Wars" bucket) and hold back the equivalent of $0.25 to $0.50 in earnings per share (EPS). The idea is that as you head into the last month of the quarter, the CMO will then check in with the CRO/CFO on the forecast. If the quarter is looking light on sales, the budget money in the escape valve can be "held back" if the company needs it to meet EPS guidance. (Being light on the top line is never great as a public company, and missing EPS guidance will put the company in the penalty box with investors—and make the stock drop.)

The inverse then applies in strong quarters. Savvy CFOs of high-growth companies do not want to over-perform their guidance by too much. Because when you overachieve, expectations change: "The company had a blowout quarter this year, now we need to have an even-more-blowout quarter next year."

So, what happens?

The CFO/CRO tells the CMO, "I need you to spend $2M in 2 weeks. Can you do that?"

How To Do Legendary Marketing At The End Of Each Quarter

When the CFO and CMO have built this approach into the plan, it means with two weeks left in the quarter the CFO can say, "We are going to blow out our sales projections. We need to spend some money."

The reason this happens is because a public company's CFO is managing dozens of different metrics, which is called "guidance." They guide the street on revenue, sales or bookings, margins, EPS, etc., all of which give investors insight into how the company is performing and, more importantly, how they can expect the company to perform in the future.

All legendary CMOs understand this, and so what they do is work closely with the CFO to wait and see how the company is doing before holding or executing their budget. If the company is light, they hold back on the marketing budget a bit to help give an internal buffer for other costs (remember, the marketing budget is the company's budget). And if the company is going gangbusters, the CFO will often tell the CMO to go to town and blow a couple million buckets in the last few weeks of the quarter.

However, in order to do this, and do it well, you have to plan for it.

Spending $2 million in 2 weeks might not sound like a hard job, but it is. And the reason is because you can't just "buy" the ads in that two-week time frame. You need to actually have $2 million dollars worth of ads run. Because even though the expense occurred in the quarter (accrual accounting), it gets counted when it *happens.* It does you no good to call up *The Wall Street Journal* and say, "We want to spend $2 million dollars on ads," and they say, "Great, we'll feather them out over the next 6 weeks."

That's not what you need.

The only way to turn your "marketing budget" into both a safety valve and a NOS button (nitrous oxide) is for the marketing department, the finance department, and both the CMO and the CFO to be on the same page. You have to be ready for it. Which means your team needs to know how to execute this strategy, and your advertising and marketing partners need to know what sort of position you're in so that you can call them with 2 weeks left in the quarter and say, "I need to run $1M in ads this week," and they can do that for you.

This is a pro tip of pro tips.

So, if you are a savvy CMO of a publicly traded company in a quarterly fiscal year, you should be all over this near the end of each quarter. In fact, you've probably already been told by the CFO how the quarter is looking, and whether the company should pull or push—hold back some of the marketing budget, or blow a couple million dollars in 10 days.

If you aren't doing this, or you've never thought to do this, we want you to send this book to your CMO or CFO right now and talk about it.

And by the way: if you (as the new CMO) walk into the CFOs office and say, "Listen, I've been thinking about this, and I have an idea for a strategy that would give us flexibility in our spend and therefore our financial performance," the CFO is going to say, "Holy-swashbuckling-hell, who are you?" Because normally this is a dumb fight between the CMO and CFO, and the source of tension between marketing folks and finance folks in large companies. It's also one of the biggest reasons

CMOs get fired—because they just keep saying, "I need more money for marketing."

Don't be that person.

Legendary CMOs partner deeply with CFOs.

When all of this is executed well, and the marketing team starts working together with the finance team, you unlock a whole new realm of possibilities for what you can do with your marketing spend. (By the way, this also helps build quality relationships between Finance and Marketing professionals, which is critical for doing legendary Investor Relations. High performance companies have the CFO and CMO working hand-in-glove.)

How To Be a Hall of Fame Marketer At the End of Your Career

Being a great CMO that your CFO loves *even just once* is an amazing accomplishment.

Of course, every great executive deep down knows that serendipity and *being in the right place at the right time* has an outsized impact on success that can't be taken credit for. Us Category Pirates raise our rum glasses to the executives who have successfully engineered success across multiple companies over different categories. To accomplish this, you have to take the art of becoming best friends with the CFO to another level.

For example:

Dwight Brown was a legendary marketing executive at Gillette, and then became the CMO at Keurig and CMO at iRobot. Dwight's marketing playbook (built on Superconsumers, marketing mix modeling, and integrated Information,

Air, and Ground War strategies) was so legendary that he, his CFO, and CEO told Wall Street they were taking earnings forecasts down so they could invest more in marketing. Billions of dollars of incremental revenue and market cap later, he was proven right each time.

CMOs like Dwight understand three important POVs that don't just make the CFO your best friend, but get you into the Hall of Fame.

1. Marketing should be a profit center, not an expense.

Marketing is more about showing, not shouting.

Dwight believed marketing budgets should not just be a spending "free for all," but a strategic test and learning exercise to experiment—where everything is measured to a statistician's satisfaction, and languaged to the delight of the Superconsumer.

Wherever Dwight went, his first two calls were to Pirate Eddie to learn about the Superconsumer, and to his favorite marketing mix modeling firm. Dwight understood marketing didn't just have to be an expense but could become a profit center.

2. Marketing should be viewed holistically beyond just mass media and digital.

Second, Dwight saw the marketing value of seemingly ancillary businesses and products.

At Keurig, he saw the true marketing and economic value of the reusable K-Cup. At face value, this product seemed like a bad idea as it was antithetical to the way Keurig made money, which was on the K-Cups (they broke even or lost a little money on the brewers). But he understood the reusable K-Cup was actually an incredible marketing vehicle to the consumer, who saw it and said, "Wow, at least this way I have a choice of using their K-Cups or my own coffee." It conveyed a sense of trust with the company that accelerated adoption.

But Dwight also knew to not underestimate the profit potential off the laziness of the American consumer. He knew many would buy the reusable K-Cup, use it once, and never use it again. As a result, he made sure it was priced high and was a high-margin product and marketing vehicle.

This was part of a broader strategy to show the consumer Keurig understood them versus shouting at the consumer via traditional marketing means. The reusable K-Cup told the consumer "We know you want variety, choice and agency." Letting Starbucks into the Keurig ecosystem was another incredibly stressful and risky decision, but Keurig knew it would tell consumers, again, Keurig understood they wanted variety, choice and agency.

Note: Starbucks chose to launch a competing single serve coffee brewer just six months after Keurig let them in the K-Cup ecosystem. Focusing on putting brewers into offices where employees could sample and try the experience for free was *showing* the benefit of Keurig, not shouting at them. Dwight understood the total experience mattered, and would be more important than just a huge advertising buy.

3. The company's business model has tremendous marketing potential.

CFOs loved and appreciated Dwight because he intimately understood the company's business model.

For Keurig, he knew the business was more like the airline business than the coffee business. When an airplane flies with an empty seat, that lost revenue is gone forever. Similarly, when a Keurig failed to work, that particular coffee drinking moment is lost.

So, in the early days of Keurig, Dwight made sure their call center and customer service had the philosophy to "kill consumers with kindness." If a brewer was out of warranty, they tended to give it a pass and replace it. And they often used FedEx to make sure the replacement brewer was there as soon as possible. This not only kept customers drinking K-Cups, it engineered goodwill that spread to other consumers.

Brewers begat brewers.

And CFOs loved Dwight because he knew precisely how their business model's bread was buttered.

Lightning Strikes: Why "Peanut Butter Marketing" Fails (And What You Should Do Instead)

Some people in marketing confuse activity and outcome.

But the truth is, no one cares how busy you are. Or how much you "do."

They care about results. And in business, you are your results.

You want to have a legendary career? Produce legendary results. And we'll tell you what the #1 result is: creating enduring value (as measured by market cap/valuation) by designing and dominating a category that matters.

We think it's wise to look at every component of a marketing plan and ask, "Does this initiative help us design and dominate a giant category that matters?" If not, why are we doing it? Remember, every "yes" comes with massive expense not just in money, but in time and focus. And a legendary marketing plan questions everything (even the premise of the entire category) and is not just about what we *are* planning on doing, but what we are planning *not* to do.

One of our favorite expressions is, "It's time to shave the dog." Which means, "It's time to take out the unnecessary." We've never seen a marketing budget that did not waste at least 10% on stupidities. (Including budgets we've been responsible for!).

So shave that doggie down.

Finally, if you are truly being strategic as a CMO (with your CFO), your marketing budget should not be evenly distributed all throughout the year.

Unfortunately, this is the marketing model that still permeates (to this day).

And it goes back to the Mad Men days of advertising.

It's called Reach & Frequency.

Many marketers today don't know the term, but the mindset is alive and well. Just listen to the asinine advice from entrepreneur hustleporn stars and you'll see what we mean. *"You gotta pump out 500 pieces of social content every day! You gotta be on all the platforms! This is an attention game! Do more, hustle, be everywhere!"*

Reach & Frequency means "the more people (reach) who see my brand, more often (frequency), the better off we'll be."

But this just ain't so.

The advertising legends of the olden days (David Ogilvy, for one) weren't successful because of Reach & Frequency strategies. They were successful because they owned a specific position in the customer's mind (which Al Ries & Jack Trout later called "Positioning"). And you do not achieve this leadership position via Reach & Frequency (aka: brand as many customers with your logo as possible). You achieve a leadership position by creating a new and different category in the customer's mind, and then moving their attention *FROM* the old category *TO* the new.

It's estimated that, back in the 70s, the average person saw between 500 and 1,600 ads per day. By 2007, that number had climbed up to 5,000 ads per day. And in 2021, it was estimated "the average person encounters between **6,000 and 10,000 ads every single day.**" This includes the brand of camera you use as your webcam, the logo on the coffee mug on your desk, the name on your T-shirt, and so on.

How is Reach & Frequency supposed to work in an environment like that?

It doesn't.

Unfortunately, companies aim to please everyone internally, and so what happens is what we like to call "peanut butter marketing." It's what happens when Reach & Frequency meets HR ("We need an employer brand!), and the company tries to give every department a little bit of marketing budget to play with (the same way you were supposed to take turns using the felt tip markers in kindergarten).

Peanut Butter Marketing = "spread it equally around."

- Equally around your departments.
- Equally around your geographies.
- Equally around your products & services.
- Equally around the 4 quarters of the year.

Want a clear signal a company treats its marketing like a service bureau, and loves Peanut Butter Marketing?
They say things like, "Marketing has internal customers."
Which is just a different way of saying: "You better give me some budget otherwise I'm going to go tell Mom."
Reach & Frequency and Peanut Butter Marketing is another easy way to get fired as a CMO.
And, more importantly, a surefire way to lose a category battle.

Moving To A Lightning Strike Model

Instead, you want to approach marketing the same way Hollywood markets movies.
Everywhere, in an instant.

All throughout the year (or several years), you don't hear a peep from Hollywood about the next Marvel movie. That's a job for Superconsumers: sharing memes on social media, blogging about hypothetical plot twists, and recreating iconic scenes on TikTok. But the week the Marvel movie comes out? If you are a fan of superhero movies, you can't go anywhere (in the real world or the digital world) without coming into contact with something Marvel related.

The movie does a LIGHTNING STRIKE!

And then, a week later, **it's over.**

And you have to wait to hear from Marvel again.

The logic here is that it's better to matter to your Superconsumers 2x per year for 2 days than to not-matter to everybody, forever. Because the reality is, nobody pays attention to Peanut Butter Marketing. It's quiet. It hums along like white noise. It never does anything legendary enough to warrant paying attention, and it never shuts up enough so that you can experience some silence (and excitement for the next time you might hear an important message). It just *lingers*.

So you either rise above the noise. Or you are the noise.

For example, this is what Apple does every year with their virtual events unveiling their newest product offerings. For these few days, you can't go anywhere online without hearing about these new Apple announcements. Photos and videos and articles about the new iPhones and iWatches, AirPods, and more are everywhere, and their Superconsumers are out in the streets carrying the message far and loud.

But after the week of their event?

Apple's lightning strike is over.

The Multiplier Effect

Don't get it confused.

A lightning strike is not an effort to try to market to "everybody."

Apple doesn't care if your grandma watches their live event. The only thing Apple cares about is that technology Superconsumers tune in.

Why?

Because you don't need "everybody" to get the category to tip at scale. You just need the Supers. You need the people most likely to a) care, and b) tell their friends why they should care. And when done correctly (putting the right words in the right mouths), you can make a million dollar marketing budget feel like $100 million.

We call this "The Multiplier Effect."

The press release multiplies the trending hashtag. The trending hashtag multiplies the DTC giveaway. The DTC giveaway multiplies the content. The content multiplies the ad campaign. And so on, and so on—all of which, when aimed directly at your Superconsumers, makes it feel as though this one company has "taken over" for a small window of time.

And that's the goal.

- If you are a B2B company, this usually means doing two lightning strikes per year.
- And if you are a B2C company, this might mean doing one lightning strike per quarter.

But no more than 4x per year.

(Otherwise, you're just Peanut Butter Marketing+.)

However, in order to do this effectively, you need to stop treating your marketing department like a service bureau and start treating it like the leadership department it's supposed to be. This requires you to invest 70% of your total budget on 2-4 lightning strikes per year. "You want to do what?!" the CFO will likely yell. Say yes, *that's right.* You want to do something legendary, for a moment, rather than something crunchy and forgettable, all the time.

Seasonal Lightning Strikes

You can take this one step further by aligning your lightning strikes with seasonal holidays.

For example, do customers buy chocolate the same way year round?

Not necessarily.

Christmas chocolate (fun candy to go in the kids' stockings) is different from Easter chocolate (easter eggs and big gooey-filled chocolate bunny rabbits), which is different from Valentine's Day chocolate (premium candy that special someone), which is different from Halloween chocolate (bought in bulk). As a result, a company like Hershey should treat each of these different times of year *radically* differently.

Which is exactly what they did.

The Story of Hershey

In the late 2000s, Hershey had been one of the top leaders in confection in the US for a while.

Their Air War and Ground War efforts were already strong. They had scale, and thus more money to spend on advertising and retail execution. But as many large market leaders have discovered, scale alone has diminishing returns.

Instead of continuing to pump more money into their traditional marketing channels, Hershey started investing heavily in Information War efforts. We know because JP Bilbrey, CEO of The Hershey Company, sought out Pirate Eddie's prior consulting firm, The Cambridge Group, to build proprietary Superconsumer data for the US confection category. Mark Henneman, then Cambridge partner, led a process called IDP (Insight Driven Performance) and built a massive data set built on proprietary consumer data on Superconsumers, detailing how and why they shop.

As Henneman dug into the work, he realized that confection wasn't one big category but many smaller categories that had wildly different contexts. The first important nuance was that everyday confection was purchased by wildly different Superconsumers with different POVs than "seasonal" confection (about 25% of the category). Everyday confection, on the other hand, was for spontaneous purchases, and generally simpler to buy because you (as the consumer) already knew what you liked and didn't like.

Seasonal confection was for others. It was a "gift." And each season was totally different.

Halloween is a "for strangers" category. You bought candy for people you didn't know and likely didn't care about. For example, Pirate Eddie's goal was to have just enough candy for the little kids to come by during the dusk hours of Halloween so he could turn off his lights and pretend to be asleep for the rowdier teens and adults. The primary driver of purchase here wasn't quality, but large piece count and variety.

Valentine's Day, on the other hand, was for the antithesis of strangers, and typically for people you loved (or were trying to love). Quantity isn't the goal so much as quality, uniqueness, and even specialty messages. Henneman built this same model for Easter, Christmas, and as many other seasonal periods as he could find—since every season was different and required its own proprietary data set.

After his team had built it, they connected it to big data and used it to drive clear activation protocols, investment strategies, and resource allocation decisions. Hershey then used this as the central nervous system to plug in data from Nielsen, Palantir, and others.

Not long after, Hershey was rated independently by a 3rd party as having the 2nd greatest information advantage within all of consumer packaged goods, ahead of much larger companies. They used this information advantage to create strikes targeted at different Supers at different times of the year.

The result was that Hershey could walk into every customer meeting with Walmart, Target, and Kroger with a massive information advantage. They used real data to identify opportunities to grow the category and had specific recommendations for what to do with shelf-space, merchandising, and price-promotion. Retailers were wowed by this data advantage and listened to what Hershey had to say.

(The data is the business.)

From then on, Hershey had 2x the category share within seasonal confection as the next nearest competitor. And from 2008 to 2010, cash flows doubled for Hershey. Within 5 years sales went up $2.5 billion dollars, and they generated an incremental $1 billion dollars in EBITDA. Most importantly, their market capitalization went up $10 billion as Wall Street increased their multiple.

Hershey had an information advantage, which meant it was worth exponentially more.

A Lightning Strike To Hijack The Holidays

How else can you hijack the holidays?

There is almost no finer example in modern history than The Macy's Day Parade.

Macy's, a department store, hijacked one of the most valuable times of year for retailers everywhere: the holiday season. Every year since the 1920s, Macy's has dominated the holidays, the parade even being broadcasted by NBC to millions of viewers. On the surface, this looks like a fun, memorable, timeless, even "American" event. But what is it, really?

It's a lightning strike.

It's a massive trade show for Macy's. Floating down the streets of Manhattan. Broadcasted live.

And people stay up all night, and stand out in the freezing cold, just to watch it.

(When thousands line up to watch your marketing, you're doing legendary marketing.)

Lightning Strikes That Hijack Moments Of The Year

Another way to approach lightning strikes is to think about what time of year you want to own in the customer's mind.

For example, Pirate Christopher remembers working with a struggling startup called Chegg in the late 2000s. The company was an education technology company focused on providing students with textbook rental, tutoring services, etc. At the time, Chegg was having a hard time raising its next round of funding—it hadn't proven itself (yet). And the company was almost out of money.

Well, Pirate Christopher (along with some of his other pirate buddies) were out swashbuckling on a pirate ship one weekend, when the topic of Chegg came up. Here were some of the most brilliant marketing minds on a boat together, drinking and spitballing ideas. The problem with Chegg was that if they waited to market to students when they started school, they'd miss their window—and the students would just buy their textbooks from the bookstore at the last minute like they always did (versus renting from Chegg). For the company to be successful, they had to change *when* students got their books and *how* they got them. (Renting, not buying). It was a tall order for a startup with very limited resources.

So they came up with the idea to create "Textbook Tuesday," the first Tuesday in August when students would be able to pre-order their textbook rentals.

Maybe you remember this day as a kid, when your parents would tell you it was time to pre-order your textbooks. Pirate Christopher and his fellow pirates created that.

In Pirate Christopher's words, "We went from not being able

to get anyone to return our calls in Silicon Valley, to investors speed-dialing us willing to back up dump trucks full of cash." Chegg went on to raise more than $200 million dollars in the following years, before going public in 2013.

Like the Macy's Day Parade, "Textbook Tuesday" became a yearly lightning strike.

"Prime Day" is another terrific example.

It's estimated that 82% of American households have an Amazon Prime membership.

Let that soak in for a second.

Eighty.... Two.... Percent.

When Amazon created "Prime Day," they were effectively encouraging all of America to participate in a nationwide shopping spree for 48 hours. Because even if you don't have a Prime membership, you probably know someone who does (82% of Americans is a lot of Americans). And if you don't have one yet, a year or two of sitting on the sidelines while Americans "shop till they drop" online sure will inspire you to get one.

"Prime Day" is now a yearly lightning strike that consumes the Internet.

And never in U.S. history has one offering from one company been in 82% of American homes. (iPhone has 47% U.S. category share by way of comparison.)

Just think about what an achievement that is.

Create Your Own Awards Ceremony (For Your Own Lightning Strike)

You can also create your own day of consequence.

This might be an event—like Salesforce's yearly Dreamforce event.

This might be a "day"—like Tesla's AI Day.

Or this might be an awards ceremony.

Back in the go-go days of the Internet, Pirate Christopher did this with Mercury. The company was working on creating a new category called Business Technology Optimization (BTO). So, what did they do? They found an exclusive VIP event in Palm Springs, California, sponsored the dinner party, and converted it into "The BTO Awards Ceremony."

Because when you give out awards, people think, "This must be a real thing."

And so it was.

This lightning strike educated an entire industry on the importance of remaining at the leading edge of Internet commerce, and ta-da: Business Technology Optimization became a category of consequence in the world of technology. The awards Mercury gave out started to mean something. "So much so that people would get up on stage and cry," said Pirate Christopher.

How To Market Like A Pirate In 2022

If you started reading this book thinking we were going to give you an excel spreadsheet, a worksheet, and a template for you to fill in to create your Ultimate Marketing Plan, we regret to inform you, you're drunk.

Our hope here is to give you a mental framework for how to *think* about doing marketing that matters. (Thinking about thinking is the most important kind of thinking.) And marketing that matters isn't "optimize your Facebook ads with these 3 easy steps" or "let's put a PR firm on retainer to get us a few press mentions per quarter." This Peanut Butter Marketing is fine to keep going in the background, but at most should only make up 30% of your total marketing budget. The rest should be spent on taking risks, launching lightning strikes, and mattering to your Superconsumers 2-4 times per year, MAX.

Anything more than that, and you aren't making lightning crash down.

And if you're doing 0 lightning strikes, then you are likely irrelevant.

What's important to remember here, however, is how little "the masses" matter in your marketing efforts. The focus of your marketing plan, almost to an obsessive degree (and purposefully exclusionary) is to speak to and attract your Superconsumers. Because if you get the Supers, you win. Simple as that.

Your goal should be to create the Comic-Con for your category—physically, virtually, whatever that means to you (and for your Supers).

6

Rethinking Black Friday & Discount Marketing

In the late 2000s, the United States ran one of the largest discounting (via couponing) experiments in entrepreneurial history.

A small startup based in Chicago came up with a radically different idea to help small businesses generate buzz, awareness, and customer acquisition. Instead of encouraging them to run ads on Facebook, or helping these small "e" entrepreneurs launch creative discounting campaigns, this startup turned the age-old marketing tactic of couponing, digital.

These digital coupons were called Groupons.

Overnight, small businesses that ran Groupons saw a huge surge in business. Hair salons, pizza parlors, physical therapy offices, and sandwich shops suddenly had lines out the door and down the street. As a result, Groupon became one of the fastest-growing startups in history, climbing to an IPO just three years after the company's founding at a jaw-dropping valuation of $13 billion (and along the way, rejecting a $6 billion acquisition offer from Google). Groupon lit the world on fire—and in the short term, seemed like the single greatest way of getting customers in the door.

10 years later, Groupon has become a thing of the past with a market cap of less than $1 billion.

What happened?

The category collapsed. Turns out flash discounts don't work.

Groupon is Black Friday all year long.

In the beginning, small "e" entrepreneurs loved running Groupon promotions because it *practically guaranteed* a mob of customers.

But after running a few Groupon promotions, these same entrepreneurs realized the vast majority of the customers that showed up to take advantage of the discount weren't the customers they wanted.

These customers:

- Were one-time buyers and weren't very likely to come back and ever pay the normal rate (and also weren't very likely to sign up for any sort of membership or loyalty program).
- Weren't appreciative Superconsumers of the discounted product or service, and instead were unappreciative consumers only there because it looked "cheap."
- Customers that only purchased when the product or service was heavily discounted, forcing businesses into a "race to the bottom" in a way that actually hurt their year-long economics—now "on the drip" and reliant on running Groupon promotions to drive revenue.

In a word: these customers sucked.

And in record time, Groupon went from being one of the most valuable startups in the world to being seen as an outdated, borderline irrelevant marketing channel. **And the company's story is a legendary lesson hiding in plain sight for marketers, entrepreneurs, and business owners:** when you play the discount game, you boost sales in the short term and ruin your business in the long term. And almost every small business owner in America tried running Groupon promotions for nearly a decade, only for the conclusion of the experiment to be: *couponing (aka discounting) doesn't work.*

Ask any hair salon or pizza parlor today if they want to run another Groupon promotion and they'll likely say, "No way."

But ask any company if they want to run a Black Friday discount promotion, and they'll likely say, "Absolutely! Everyone else is discounting themselves—we should too!"

They're the same thing.

Couponing = Discounting

Discounting = Couponing

> *By the way, there's a chance Google's acquisition of Groupon might have made the company work. Google may have been able to connect the data gathered by Groupon, connect it to their flywheel—"This person has searched for this type of thing 20 times in the past month but never bought, let's give them a Groupon and get them in the door"—and used data + discounting as a way of generating net-new demand among the right kind of consumers: Superconsumers. So, to be clear, we're not anti-discounting. We're against discounting*

> *that does not attract potential Supers. Then, using the Super of 1 is a Super of 9 framework, Google could have leveraged that data again to present Groupon promotions to Superconsumers who didn't even know they would be interested in other tangentially relevant products, services, and categories. This could have revolutionized digital marketing. Imagine being in the consideration stage of buying something. You Google the category "carbadigulator" and up comes a 15% off "Groupon." Might that tip you into buying? Even if it tipped 1%, Google + Groupon could have helped to increase the revenue of millions of small businesses. Oh well. Nevermind.*

Groupon's story is a cautionary tale to companies that blindly discount their goods & services.

Every year, Black Friday comes around. And every year, big and small companies all over the world enter a zombie-like state of transactional discounting (and transactional discounting is doomed to failure) opposed to relational discounting, which allows you to build direct relationships with your Superconsumers.

One is a coupon, the other is an intentional experience.

Same cost, different context.

(And context is everything.)

Which is why we would like to give you a DIFFERENT lens for thinking about Black Friday, discounting, couponing, and short-term marketing promotions.

Reject The Premise: How To Transform Your Black Friday Promotion From A Discount To A Gift

During the busiest shopping season of the year, do you want to do *what most people do?*

Or do you want to do something DIFFERENT?

If you start with, "I reject what Black Friday stands for," you may work your way back and end up accepting the premise ("Couponing works!"), or you may end up accepting part of the premise ("Couponing works if we also do XYZ along with it"). But one thing is for certain: if you start with the thinking, "Black Friday is important; Black Friday is when everyone makes money; and the thing to do on Black Friday is to offer a huge discount," you aren't going to stand out, and more importantly, you aren't going to drive any meaningful outcomes for your business.

All you're doing is playing a game called: "Whoever sells the most TVs, wins."

Here are a few other reasons to reject the premise of Black Friday. There are a few origin stories of the phrase "Black Friday"—from two post Civil-War gold speculators in 1869, to the 1950s after an Army-Navy football game on Thanksgiving when mobs broke into and looted stores in Philadelphia. But most people understand Black Friday to be a retailer driven concept where profit starved retailers (*typical retail margins are in the low-to-mid single digits*) chase the hope of squeezing out an annual profit as they finally cover their fixed costs by November, and hope to drive a truckload of sales at deep discounts to end the year "in the black."

It boggles the mind how a not-so-clever retailer promotional tactic has gained such widespread adoption by businesses who aren't retailers. We could understand businesses falling in love with a promotional tactic inspired by Google's search business (a magnificent and remarkable business) or say a cash cow like Geico. But note that neither of these companies offer a Black Friday promotion, as far as we know.

Instead of blanket discounting, we encourage you to ask a series of more thoughtful questions:

- "What's the real outcome we want to drive? Is it revenue? Is it lead generation? If we run a coupon promotion and capture a ton of leads, will those leads be the ones we want?" (Remember the Glengarry leads?)
- "Do we want to leverage Black Friday to capture existing demand or create net-new demand?"
- "How can we use Black Friday as not just an opportunity to generate short-term revenue, but also build our category over the long term?"
- "Is there a radical stunt that we could pull off to drive home our POV?"

For example, do you know what brand your TV is?

Is it a Samsung? LG? Sony?

Chances are, you don't know *and don't care.* Last Black Friday, you went shopping for a TV and saw one of them was marked so far down that you felt you would be doing yourself a disservice if you didn't click that *Buy It Now* button and have it shipped express to your house. But now, put yourself in the shoes of whichever brand sold you that TV. Did the brand do anything that furthered your conviction in their products? Did the brand use the promotion to build a relationship with you, the customer? Did the brand, in any way, shape, or form, turn you into an enthusiast for the category?

Not really. They sold you a TV.

So sure, they moved some stuff off a truck and made a buck (probably a small amount of money, and some companies lose money on "loss leaders"). But what's the likelihood you come back and decide to buy more stuff in the future? Hard to be a repeat buyer if you don't even know what brand sold you the thing to begin with!

This is what makes mindless discounting, couponing, and conventional Black Friday marketing so ineffective.

Black Friday is transactional.

Legendary businesses are relational.

Rethinking Promotion & Pricing

Pricing is not meant to be a "gotcha" game.

When customers see you massively discounting your products and services for one or two days per year, they have two reactions:

1. "If you could always sell it at this price, how come you are charging so much the rest of the year?"

AND…

2. "Every year, I know a ton of companies will run huge Black Friday discounts. So instead of buying things now, at full rate, I'll just wait until it's 75% off and buy it then."

(This is called "training your customers to do the one thing you wished they would not do.")

Both of these outcomes are not great for you or the customer.

For you, **the brand**, it creates a vicious cycle where you train customers to only buy when there's a discount, and **for the**

customer, it deprives them of the thing you say is valuable and meaningful to them—until a day like Black Friday. They have to wait months and months to buy something they want or need because, *they can't rationalize buying it *now** when they know it will be marked down 50% a few months later.

Consumer Packaged Goods (CPG) companies, many of whom are supposedly amazing at brand building, marketing and understanding consumers (like P&G), are some of the worst culprits. According to McKinsey, 20% of CPG industry revenue goes to "trade promotions." CPG is roughly $635 billion dollars in revenue globally. So nearly $130 billion dollars are spent on trade promotions every year. That is about the same size as Chevron's revenue that is spent each year on promotion that, in theory, could fall to the bottom line. At an 8x multiple, and you get roughly $1 trillion dollars of market capitalization.

Of course, you might say CPG companies know what they are doing, right?

Not really.

Globally, 59% of trade promotions lose money. In the US, 72% of trade promotions lose money.

Which is why now you see brands running marketing campaigns in September, October, and early November trying to educate customers: "The price you see today *is* the Black Friday price." This is an attempt to unhook people's minds from assuming *every single product on planet earth* will be massively discounted one day per year. They're trying to pull the Black Friday demand forward, and tell people, "No! Don't wait! Buy it now, because this is as good as it's going to get!"

All of this is the wrong way of thinking about couponing, discounts, and short-term marketing promotions.

Don't just sell products. Build the category.

First of all, pricing should be used as a form of category differentiation.

You should either be priced so cheap (and provide so much value) that there's no need to discount. Ever.

Or, you should be priced so expensive that you are seen as "luxury" and "premium," and no luxury, premium, ultra-ding-dong brand ever discounts themselves. (When was the last time you saw a "Buy One, Get One Free" Gucci ad?)

Your pricing strategy should not be an arbitrary number plucked out of thin air. It also should not be a number based on the context of "what everyone else charges." Pricing should be a lever of category differentiation, further signaling to customers who you are, what category you're in, and what you stand for (like YETI's $1,300 super-duper-grizzly-bear-proof premium coolers.)

Second, the entire purpose of any marketing campaign is not to just "sell products."

The purpose of every marketing campaign should be to build the category and your leadership position in it.

This is the framing that matters. But instead, most marketers, entrepreneurs, executives, and business owners rush to the tactic: "What's the campaign? What's the gimmick? What's the discount? What's the promotion? BUY, BUY, BUY!" (When was the last time you saw Patagonia, Apple, or Tesla do that?)

OK, yes, but to what end?

Remember: thinking about thinking is the most important kind of thinking.

The number one way to build your category (and your leadership position in it) is to do relational marketing—specifically with your Superconsumers. Remember, Supers are not one-time buyers. Supers are people who are so emphatic about the category (or have the potential to be educated to the point of loyalty and enthusiasm) that they not only want one type of product or service, but a variety of other products and services within the overarching category. For example, if you are a Superconsumer of Pokémon memorabilia, you don't just want Pokémon plushie toys, but also Pokémon posters, onesies, and vintage collectable cards. As a result, the lifetime value (LTV) of your Superconsumers is likely to be 2x to 10x+ higher than regular consumers. (And Supers can be legendary co-designers and evangelists of the category and your brand. If you enable them.)

The way you tap into your Superconsumers and turn their enthusiasm into a multiplier effect for your business is by putting the right words (Languaging for the category) in the right mouths (your Supers). This is what allows your current Supers to educate their friends and family members and recruit (or convert) new Supers into your category—and on and on the flywheel spins.

Black Friday is about gluttony. We encourage you to make your Black Friday marketing efforts about radical gratitude & giving.

There's something ironic about how the biggest firesale of the year is the day after the United States gives thanks for the things we already have.

This scarcity "me, me, me" FOMO mentality is what leads to stampedes at Best Buy, car crashes in the parking lot of Target, and fights, stabbings, and shootings over big screen TVs and video game consoles. So much so, there's even a website now that tracks the deaths and injuries that occur on Black Friday.

That's not what being a category pirate is about.

We reject this premise of FOMO and treating your customers like buffoons who (if you discount your products and services enough) will buy regardless of whether they actually want or need the thing you're selling. Because when you treat your customers like they're sugar-addicted children, then that's your brand. And after a few years of heavy discounting, you go from being a once beloved high-quality brand to being seen as a budget alternative customers may (or may not) buy once a year, and that's it.

So, sure, you might get some sales.

But have you *built* your business? Or did you just capture some temporary demand from a customer who doesn't even know the difference between your TV and everyone else's TV?

This is the same idea we presented with entrepreneurs who unknowingly join "the brand cult": Most people's response to the problem "we're not differentiated" isn't to "get differentiated." It's to just yell louder, MAKE THE LOGO BIGGER, and discount. Well, the more comparable you are, the more replaceable you are. And the more replaceable you are, the more you need to offer some kind of incentive to "BUY NOW!"

Black Friday discounts solve that problem in the short term.

But they exacerbate the "we're not different" problem in the long term.

So, here are some ways you can get DIFFERENT this Black Friday.

4 Ways To Promote DIFFERENT Offers To Customers

There are 3 ways to drive revenue for your business.

- Target a different type of customer (one who spends more than other types of customers)
- Find ways to provide more units per customer (expand the category design and add additional products, services, and consumption models by framing, naming, and claiming more new problems that increase LTV)
- Increase the price per unit (provide more value, or change the perception of the value, to warrant a higher price)

This is the algebra of revenue. And if you can use Black Friday and other marketing holidays to create a "DIFFERENT" at each level, then that's a campaign worth running.

Unfortunately, most Black Friday promotions do the opposite:

- Discount campaigns target the wrong "different" type of customer (a one-time, cheap buyer versus a Superconsumer)

- Discount campaigns sell less units per customer (someone buys a product just because it's marked down. What they don't do is buy 5 of them—1 for themselves, and 4 for their friends—because they're in love with the product)
- And discount campaigns decreases the price per unit (cutting your economics to shreds)

All of this is important context to keep in mind before even beginning to think about the creative ways you can stand out and promote DIFFERENT offers on Black Friday (or on any other day in the year).

1. Reject the premise and say the opposite.

In 2011, Patagonia ran one of the greatest Black Friday campaigns in marketing history.

The ad, which they ran in *The New York Times* and paired with an entire POV and manifesto of their category was called, "Don't Buy This Jacket."

> *"We're placing the ad in the Times because it's the most important national newspaper and considered the "paper of record." We're running the ad on Black Friday, which launches the retail holiday season. We should be the only retailer in the country asking people to buy less on Black Friday."*

What makes this campaign work is it's starting in a fundamentally different place than every other Black Friday campaign. It takes the premise, "Black Friday is about buying more," and says the opposite: "This Black Friday, we encourage you to buy less." And because this line of thinking is aimed in the opposite direction of the status quo, it's hard to not see it, pay attention to it, remember it, want to talk about it, and even have an opinion about it—and that's the point. (And with this radically different lightning strike on Black Friday, Patagonia created a deep emotional bond with its Supers by supplanting its needs for their category mission.)

How many outdoor jacket manufacturers and brands run Black Friday sales and discounts?

Probably 99%.

But only 1 company runs a full-page ad in the *New York Times* that says "Don't Buy This Jacket" and presents people with DIFFERENT thinking: "This holiday season, think before you buy. Save the planet."

Patagonia.

2. Change the "give to get" for customers.

Black Friday was a promotional holiday created by big retail.

Retail businesses have high fixed costs and razor thin margins entirely based on how much you can sell within a certain amount of square footage. It's called "Black Friday" because it's the one day per year these extremely inefficient businesses can juice short-term profits, get "in the black" on their P&L, and in the final months of the year turn a profit.

So why would smart executives in category after category decide to emulate businesses that only make money for 1.5 months a year? *"YEAH! THAT'S IT! Our strategy is to do what some of the least effective businesses in the world do. Excellent idea, Jim!"*

But, that's exactly what happened.

And now, Black Friday is used by non-retail businesses all over the world.

(Didn't our mothers teach us just because "everyone" else does it, does not make it smart?)

One of the most prestigious strategy consulting firms ran an internal study asking the question, "Should we, one of the most prestigious consulting firms, ever consider offering a discount?" So they did the work and looked at the math internally. And the conclusion of the study was that a discount is only worth providing IF there is a very clear "give to get"—meaning what this consulting firm would "give up" in cash now, they must "get" in connections, opportunities, and cash later.

So, what's the "give to get" you can offer customers?

- Can you offer a discount IF the customer also refers a friend?
- Can you offer a discount IF the customer posts about their purchase on social media (amplifying your brand to more new customers)?
- Can you offer a free add-on or secondary product IF the customer takes a survey or quiz (allowing you to gather more data about your customers & Superconsumers)?
- Can you provide exclusive access to something extremely valuable IF a customer has been a loyal subscriber for more than a year?

Instead of just thinking about discounting or marketing campaigns as one-off promotions, how can you give more value to your customers *now* but also receive something (referrals, data, etc.) that helps build your business *long into the future.*

Do give up a "give" without getting a "get."

3. Bundle your products together to entice Superconsumers.

One-off customers buy one-off products.

But Superconsumers of a category buy multiple products, multiple times. (And they gift 'em too.)

Instead of just blanket discounting your products individually, bundle your most-popular products together to create a whole new product. For example, best-selling author Ryan Holiday has written a handful of books on the topic of Stoicism. Well, one-off buyers might buy one of his books if they see it on a discount rack while shopping. But a Superconsumer of Stoicism and reading is likely to see the boxed set—The Way, The Enemy, And The Key–and think, "Oh, I want that." (And buy 3 books instead of 1.)

This is also what makes franchise content assets so valuable. For example, there are a lot of ways to package, price, and monetize everything James Bond. That's why Amazon paid $8.45 billion for MGM.

And because the customer is buying more of your products at once, sure, you can give them a discount. Microsoft famously did this with the launch of Microsoft Office: product, pricing, and category innovation.

But the real reason bundling is so important isn't just because you end up "selling more products," but because *the type of customer* you are attracting is likely not a one-off buyer—and instead is a Superconsumer of your category. Which means you can now begin to build a relationship with them, and ideally sell them more of what they want long into the future.

Another way of thinking about bundling is grouping offers together to change the perception of what it is the customer is buying.

For example, most B2B SaaS companies are on a fiscal calendar. And for B2B companies, Q4 is where a scary amount of the sales and bookings take place. For some companies, 50% of the year's revenue comes from sales closed in the final 2-3 months of the year. If you are a SaaS executive, you hate New Year's Eve. Why? Because you aren't drinking champagne smooching your honey—you're on the phones with customers helping sales reps close deals, desperately trying to figure out where the quarter is going to land.

Now, for a B2B SaaS company, running a "Buy 2 CRMs, Get 1 CRM FREE!" campaign doesn't make a whole lot of sense.

But what *does* make sense is bundling your high-ticket offering with a low-ticket offering that is a) a value-add to customers, but more importantly b) a reason to engage in sales conversations sooner. For example, user conferences are huge in the B2B world now. So one idea might be to run a special offer where sales reps say, "If you close your Q4 deal with us by Thanksgiving, we'll give you 3x as many free passes to next year's user conference."

Now, let's not be stupid: obviously a $5M enterprise deal with a major corporation isn't going to come down to how many free passes they get to next year's industry party. BUT, what a campaign like this does is give your entire army of sales reps a reason to call all your Q4 prospects early and assess the likelihood of whether or not this prospect is actually going to pull the trigger.

All of which allows company executives to have even more

clarity and insight on which deals have the highest probability of closing—and where they should spend the majority of their time.

4. Use gifting to get your products in the hands of Superconsumers.

Don't think, "How can we sell more by charging less?"

Think, "How can we charge the same, but offer more, to sell more?"

One very basic way of doing this is to ask your Superconsumers to gift your product to people they think would also love this sort of thing (and if you love Category Pirates, we would love it if you gifted someone else a subscription!). Because if you are passionate about something, chances are you want to talk about it, you want to share it with the people in your life, and you want other people to "drink the Kool-Aid" and share the experience with you.

All you have to do is ask your Superconsumers.

To be clear: discounting can work. We are just encouraging you to do so strategically.

If your goal is to run a discount targeted at potential Superconsumers to get them introduced to your product or service, great.

There's some validity to that.

But again, we want you to ask the question: to what end?

Are you using discounting to win a comparison game? Have you unknowingly fallen into The "Better" Trap? Are you blindly fighting for short-term revenue?

Or are you using Black Friday (and other "marketing holidays") to be provocative, innovative, and creative such that you bring attention to the CATEGORY and the problem you believe needs solving in the world? And are you executing a Dam The Demand strategy such that others consider you, first—not at the product level, but the category level?

As it stands, Black Friday is primarily about capturing existing demand.

Which again, is fine. But don't be confused: you just moved a few more TVs off the truck, and that's it.

(Did we learn anything from Groupon?)

What you didn't do was expand the category, evangelize the problem, empower your Superconsumers, educate & convert potential customers into new Superconsumers, or create any real brand affinity that further establishes yourself as the category leader.

All you did was give customers a discount.

7

How To Create Content That Matters

In today's digital age, "content is king."

On January 27th, 2021, we published our first Category Pirates newsletter. Us three pirates had been working on a book together for almost two years. But after several drafts and many rewrites, it became clear we weren't really writing one long book—we were writing dozens of mini-books. And we felt, instead of trying to cram all the information together into one big dense stack of paper, our readers would be better off consuming these ideas, frameworks, and new ways of thinking about category design piece by piece, week by week, digitally.

All three of us have written conventional books and read many books ourselves.

But we realized that we Pirates should drink our own rum and follow our own treasure map.

For example, the book category has a lot of good components. We each have books we love. We have books that have transformed our careers and lives. And we owe a tremendous debt of gratitude to those books. But the book category also has a lot of bad components. Too many books are *one great idea* spread out across 200-300 pages that leave the reader feeling like they were continually "Rick-Rolled" after that one great chapter. We wish these books came with a preface written by the editor of the book under truth serum that said, "Psst…we love this idea, but just read pages 33-70 and you'll get the gist. You can skip the rest."

The book category also has a lot of ugly components. The book publishing business model today takes as much risk as a venture capital firm but with much less upside. Like startups, the vast majority of books will "fail," while even the most financially successful books & authors in the world (the J.K. Rowlings and James Pattersons) achieve a fraction of high-flying unicorns.

This broken risk/reward model causes publishers to hunt for books to acquire and publish in a more mercenary fashion. Most of the questions they have are "How are you going to help us sell enough of these books to cover the risk of our first printing?" as opposed to "How will this book change the world for the better?" And book retailers seem like a noble business, until you realize how little risk they take on the authors and publishers by returning unsold books and getting full refunds.

The entire industry is so busy playing hot potato with the risks that come with book publishing that too many have lost the mission of transforming lives through the written word.

From our perspective, the legacy category of "big book publishing" is dying.

So, we abandoned our long-form book project and started a Substack weekly newsletter instead. (Will we still write long-form books? Of course. *You're reading one right now!* But we are a digital-first, 100% independent, publishing company.)

Less than a year later, Category Pirates has become one of the Top 10 paid business newsletters on the platform.

Here's why now is the perfect time to start your own (free or paid) business newsletter for yourself and/or your business:

There are a handful of tailwinds accelerating the newsletter category.

1. Direct To Creator: Substack is one of many platforms working hard to give creators the tools they need to build (and monetize) their audiences directly. Other platforms like Gumroad, Patreon, OnlyFans, etc., have been working to support Direct To Creator relationships for a while now (Gumroad was founded in 2011, Patreon in 2013, and OnlyFans in 2016), with Substack being the most recent to enter the fast-moving macro category of Direct To Creator platforms. As these capabilities become more prevalent, it's safe to assume that having a direct relationship with your audience will soon become a bare-minimum expectation for creators & business owners (opposed to purely leveraging rented audiences on social platforms). Further, as Direct To Creator expands, more and more consumers will come to expect this direct relationship with their trusted sources. Like all new category designs, it will shift from being viewed as an innovation to a *must have* over time.

2. Bottoms-Up Iteration Models: The internet has made it very easy to gather data on what people are most interested in, what questions they have, and what they find most valuable. One of the frameworks Pirate Cole shares with other writers in his digital writing program, Ship 30 for 30, is how to test and validate ideas before choosing which ones to invest in. For example, instead of committing to writing a long-form book, create a course, or launch a product *day one*, it's much better to start small, leverage rapid-fire feedback loops, gather reader/audience data, and iterate as you go. Newsletters, as well as other digital writing social platforms (Twitter, Medium, Quora, etc.) can be great ways to learn who your Superconsumers are and where you can provide them with the most value. Which means, by the time you decide to write a book, create a course, or launch your own product/service/business, you should already know whether you're building/writing the right thing. This is the new way to create products and launch businesses, and anyone not making use of these rapid-fire feedback loops is going to get left in the dust.

3. Paywalls: Substack was founded in 2017. Their mission was to give writers the ability to charge their audiences directly for access to their content—and as a result, created the "paid newsletter" category. Even just a few years ago, launching a paid newsletter was extremely difficult. And if you wanted one, you had to Duct-tape a handful of different tools together and figure out how to make it work on your own (and the same was true for almost any kind of paywall). But from 2017 and through the pandemic in 2020, paywalls have become significantly more popular, more accepted, and more accessible. Creators of every kind can easily paywall their content today—whether it's writing via Substack, or videos via OnlyFans. And as digital privacy becomes more important, and the unintended consequences of social media advertising become more prevalent (as seen with Facebook), the tailwind behind paywalled content is only going to accelerate.

4. Demand For Analog "Stuff" Is Going Down: While physical book sales are holding strong (and still generate ~75% of the revenue in the book publishing industry), ebook sales are continuing to climb. We have written in the past about Native Analogs vs Native Digitals and how, as Millennials and Gen-Zers get older, demand for Analog "stuff" is likely to go down (fast). And as Pirates, we like making decisions that bet on the future being DIFFERENT and allow us to capitalize on that DIFFERENT future when it arrives. If Analog products are facing heavy headwinds, and there are strong tailwinds behind Digital products, then now is the best time to start investing in building digital value, with digital-first audiences, who love consuming and sharing your digital products.

Whether you are a business owner, a creator, a company executive, or a writer, don't be confused: newsletters, *as a category*, might be "saturated," but **valuable newsletters** known for a specific niche will never be.

We want to share with you how, in less than a year, we built Category Pirates into a Top 1% (paid) business newsletter, so that you can leverage the above tailwinds and do the same.

1. Have A Radically Different Point Of View

People don't read newsletters.
 People don't buy products.
 People don't buy books, courses, plastic widgets, or journals.
 What people buy is *access to information.*
 Different. Valuable. Information.
 They buy treasure maps for specific parts of their lives.

- Business treasure maps to help them succeed in their careers.
- Relationship treasure maps to help them transform their marriages and relationships with their parents, children, and friends.
- Cooking treasure maps to help them find the perfect pie recipe that will make next Thanksgiving even more memorable.

The medium in which you communicate this information is almost irrelevant. If we said to you, "We know you are experiencing this very specific, very painful problem, and we know how you can solve it in an instant—*but the only way we can send you the information is by carrier pigeon...*" you would shout, "WELL THEN SEND THE DAMN PIGEON!"
 Now, is it beneficial to make use of macro-category tailwinds and utilize new mediums of communication?
 Absolutely.
 But the medium comes second to the message. (With all due respect to Marshall McLuhan.)

Product-First Mindset vs Category-First Mindset

The single point of failure for every business, every product, every service, every social media post, and every newsletter is your Point Of View.

- If you are sharing a different POV, you have a fighting chance.
- If you are not sharing a different POV, and are just trying to say the same thing as everyone else in your category/industry but "better," you've already lost.

Most writers, creators, marketers, entrepreneurs, and businesses (big and small) approach content creation through a product-first mindset. "How can we make our newsletter *better* than the competition? How can we be *smarter*? How can we utilize *more research*? How can we publish *more content, more often*—how can we be *faster*?" What they fail to realize, however, is that no matter how much better/faster/smarter/cheaper they make their content, they are still firmly positioned in someone else's shadow. Someone else is the Category King, and they are just another hungry squire trying to steal a few loaves of bread from the kingdom.

Meanwhile, the products, services, and businesses that catch fire are the ones with a category-first mindset.

They don't differentiate by trying to be "better." *They change the premise of the conversation.* For example, if you are in the financial services industry, there are gazillions of newsletters that give readers stock recommendations, startup investing tips, etc. Trying to do this same thing, "better," is a loser's strategy. So what entrepreneur Codie Sanchez did, for example, was present readers with a different point of view: "Don't buy stocks and don't try to chase high-flying startups. Instead? **Buy boring businesses.**"

Radically different POV = radically different product and value proposition.

So, how do you get out of The "Better" Trap and come up with a unique, new, and different POV?

Here are a few ways to get started.

You can change the subject of the category.

In the above example, what makes Codie Sanchez's newsletter "different" is that she changed the subject (the "premise") of the category. She's still writing within the macro category of finance & investing, but *the thing* she is talking about within that category (her "niche") is different. Lots of people write about picking stocks. But who else writes about **how to buy boring businesses that produce healthy cash flows?**

The key here is to get hyper-specific about what it is you're actually writing about. Is it "business news" in general? Or is it news updates on *small* businesses? Or *remote* businesses?

The more specific you can get about the subject you are writing about, the easier it is for readers to decide (in a very binary way) whether this is *exactly* for them, or *exactly not* for them. The most powerful way to start is with a micro category/niche. Then, once you become known for a niche you own, you can expand out from there.

You can change the outcome of the category.

Another way to differentiate your content is to change the outcome you are promising readers.

For example, notice the difference between an investing

newsletter that promises readers stock recommendations that will make them a lot of money (outcome #1) versus an investing newsletter that promises to teach readers how to navigate emerging cryptocurrency laws (outcome #2). By changing the outcome you are helping the reader achieve, you are likely moving out of one category of subject matter and into another.

How do you reverse-engineer this?

Focus on solving a *different* problem.

If everyone else is focused on creating content around "hiring best practices," how can you write about (and solve) a different and even more specific problem? Maybe readers don't actually want hiring best practices. Maybe the more pressing problem they're experiencing is a problem called, "I don't know what interview questions to ask," and your weekly newsletter is nothing but the most effective interview questions to use for different hires, at different levels of the organization, sourced from the most effective managers at large, fast-growing companies.

Woah, that's *different!*

You can also change the audience of the category.

Finally, you can niche down even further by changing who the content is for.

Notice the differences:

- Investing 101 For Teenagers
- Investing 101 For College Students
- Investing 101 For First-Time Parents
- Investing 101 For Late Bloomers & Boomers

Just by changing the intended audience, you can radically change which category you are in (and also, by definition, changes the Subject and the Outcomes you write about). There is so much untapped potential in writing for audiences who *aren't* being served and creating content custom-tailored for them—opposed to trying to create "better" content in an existing category for an audience that is already being served to the point of gluttony.

Specificity is the secret.

The overarching takeaway we want you to have here is that the more specific you can be about what you're writing about, what outcome(s) you want your readers to achieve, and who your readers are, the more differentiated you'll be.

Conversely, the biggest mistake content creators, writers, artists, and even business owners make is trying to be everything to everyone. They pick big, broad categories ("Business Advice") and make the conscious decision NOT to get specific because they *"don't want to alienate any readers."*

But in trying to write something for everyone, they end up writing something for no one.

2. Bring Fresh Data, Frameworks, And Insights

If readers can easily find your ways of solving problems elsewhere, you are not writing differentiated content.

This is something all the Tier 2 business publications do—and it has forced them into a race to the bottom. *Inc Magazine* publishes the same tools, tips, insights, and survey findings as *Forbes*, as *Fortune*, as *Business Insider*, as <fill in the blank>. As a result, you (the reader) don't really care where you get the information. You Google your question, and then you click on whichever link is closest to the top. You have no loyalty to any of these publications.

There are only a handful of publications that are known for bringing fresh data, frameworks, and insights to the table. *Harvard Business Review* is one of them. *The Economist* is another. For news, *The New York Times* and the *Wall Street Journal*. For "think pieces," *The New Yorker, The Atlantic*. But most of the others blur together. In fact, we would argue that if the logo was removed from the top of the page, you would have no idea whether you were reading *Inc Magazine, Forbes,* or *The Huffington Post.*

And that's a big problem.

> *We can think of very few categories where the products and brands are so literally interchangeable that even Superconsumers can not tell them apart. Nothing legendary is generic.*

How To Present Fresh Data

Data is the hardest way to differentiate because it usually takes the most time, energy, and money to create.

If you want to go down this path and differentiate your content based on unique, original data, your entire content creation process is going to be centered around running/funding studies, conducting surveys, pulling research, etc. Remember: publications like *The New York Times* and the *Wall Street Journal* have entire departments dedicated to this stuff. It's a heavy lift.

Another way to present fresh data, however, is to share survey findings and research someone else (a major publication) took the time to gather *but interpret the data through a different lens.* For example, in Category Pirates we rarely (if ever) go conduct our own surveys. But what we will do is take a set of data points published by other reputable sources and then dissect them **through a category lens**. This presents fresh thinking to readers, and allows them to see the data from a different perspective or vantage point than they might have otherwise.

A third way to present fresh data is to pull findings from unconventional industries or categories. For example, if your newsletter is all about the future of B2B practices, pulling data from that world probably isn't going to be seen as new and different. But if you were to present data from the music industry, or the NFT category, and cross-reference that data with more commonly accepted B2B industry data to present readers with new conclusions, that would be seen as *different.*

How To Create New Frameworks

A framework is a lens, a way of shaping context in an effort to change thinking in a unique, different way. If you have ever said, "I never thought about it that way!" you've experienced trying on a different *framing of thinking.*

Anyone can create a framework.

In fact, we would argue that the more frameworks you can Frame, Name, and Claim, the more likely you are to become known for a niche you own.

Almost all best-selling nonfiction authors do this. They take a concept, break it into steps, give that framework a "name," and voila. Here are some examples:

- *Thinking, Fast and Slow:* Daniel Kahneman did something legendary with this book. He took two modes of thinking (that have been well known, well researched, and well documented long before his writing this book) and called them something. One way of thinking is "fast." The other way of thinking is "slow." **Wabam**. The Naming & Claiming of this idea and new way of seeing the world led to a best-selling book and almost 3 million copies sold. (Do not underestimate the power of Languaging.)
- *Atomic Habits:* The subtitle of James Clear's best-selling book says it all. *An Easy & Proven Way To Build Good Habits & Break Bad Ones.* What is this? A framework. A way of solving X by doing Y.
- *How To Win Friends & Influence People:* Arguably one of the most influential self-help/pop-business books ever written, this book changed the way people thought about "networking." But what is the book, really? It's just Carnegie walking readers through frameworks based on his own personal experiences: "6 ways to make people like you. 12 ways to win people to your way of thinking. 9 ways to change people without arousing resentment." (Lists are frameworks people love.)

The truth is, anyone can create a framework. It's not something that is only reserved for gurus and Nobel Prize winners.

And the way you create a framework is very simple. We're going to show you how by using: *A Pirate's Framework For Creating Frameworks.* (See how we Framed, Named & Claimed this!)

Step 1: Take anything you have figured out how to do successfully in your life or business and break it apart into steps.

For example: maybe you've become an all-star sales rep over the years and now you want to help other sales reps learn how to close deals like you do.

To create a framework for readers (aka: other sales reps), the first thing you need to do is slow down your thinking. Sure, you've gotten good at closing deals, but the process has probably become automatic. You operate off experience and instinct at this point. Which means, in order to help get other people up to speed, you need to get out of "automatic" mode and back into "manual mode." (This takes real thinking. Transforming from Player to Teacher is no easy feat. Remember Bleacher Report questioning if Michael Jordan was the worst basketball owner ever?)

Start by breaking the entire interaction down into steps:

- How do you find sales leads? (*This, by itself, can also be a framework.*)
- What's the best way to reach out to a cold lead vs a warm lead? (*This can also be its own framework.*)
- What do your email follow-ups look like? (*And this can be its own framework.*)
- And so on.

Get specific about what needs to be done in each step so that the reader has all the information they need in order to move forward on their own. Again, specificity is the secret.

Here's a quick example from Pirate Eddie's consulting

business.

Early in his career, Pirate Eddie was trying to build a relationship with a senior executive of a multi-billion dollar food business. The only problem was he had nothing in common with this executive. Pirate Eddie's boss at the time said, "Let's get our wives together and all go out for a four-hour, fine-dining French cuisine dinner with endless bottles of expensive wine." And all Pirate Eddie—an extreme introvert, married to another extreme introvert—could think was how incredibly painful of an experience this was going to be.

Some years later, Pirate Eddie's new boss, who was a senior partner at McKinsey for many years, gave him some freeing advice **and a framework that changed his career.** Pirate Eddie was told to not feel compelled to spend time with clients that he didn't click with. It's not that some clients are bad people or Eddie was a bad partner, but the combination didn't work and that was okay. "Plus, if you spend time with someone you don't click with, you'll hate your work and quit—or more likely, the other person will be able to tell you don't click with them and you'll come across as a fake mercenary," his boss said.

This helped Pirate Eddie breathe a sigh of relief. But it also made him worry about his performance as a partner. So Pirate Eddie was given the 2-4-8 framework.

- A successful consulting partner would have at least two active projects/clients at any given time. If you spend most of your time on those **2**, and ensure those achieve grand slam outcomes, they will become repeat clients—and repeat clients are the lifeblood of any successful partner.
- In addition, try to have **4** active proposals at any given time. These should have a clear view of the problem you're

trying to solve, how the scope solves that problem, and a price tag that is a fraction of the marketplace impact you expect to have for your client, but is much bigger than your costs and makes you feel good about your contribution to the firm.
- Most importantly, have **8** active conversations with senior clients. These are NOT proposal discussions nor are the commercial in any real way. These are open-ended, no-agenda conversations about their business, your own business, someone else's business, or business overall. The purpose of these conversations is to "nerd out" over business, learn, and have fun! When there is no whiff of a hard sell, senior executives are always happy to talk because they don't feel treated like a transaction. These active conversations should be beneficial for both parties, as each learns new things, marvels over industry successes, and winces together at industry car crashes. These are conversations between missionaries, not mercenaries. Over time, trust builds. Credibility grows. And when that senior client does have a need, they will shift gears from the "8" part of the framework to the "4" part of the framework and eventually become part of the "2".

This framework changed Pirate Eddie's career—and more importantly, his life.

So, getting back to your framework...

If your steps present vague information like, "Step 1: Reach out and be yourself," the reader is going to be left feeling confused, deprived, and upset. It's not helpful to tell readers, "Just do it." You have to literally say to them: "First, do this. Second, do this—and if you need help doing this, try this." Give them the "it" in Just Do It! The more detail you can provide, the better. And the more questions you can proactively answer, the more the reader is going to want to bookmark, save, and re-read your content over and over again.

Step 2: Name & Claim each step.

Giving someone the answer isn't enough.

The way the answer (or the step, the insight, the framework) *sticks* is by calling it something. The difference between "livestock" and pets? Names. Names humanize. Names make things relatable and memorable. If it's important, it has a name. This should be done on the micro level (each step) and the macro level (all the steps combined). Building on the above example, notice the differences between unclaimed steps vs Named & Claimed steps.

Unclaimed Steps:

- "First, find sales leads."
- "Second, reach out to cold leads by calling them, and warm leads by emailing them."
- "Third, follow up via email."

Named & Claimed Steps:

- Step 1: The Infinity Sales Leads Generator
- Step 2: The Cold Lead, Warm Lead Situation Matrix
- Step 3: Instant Response Follow-Up Email Templates

There is something so gratifying for readers about having each step, each insight, each meaningful milestone along the way neatly organized. It's easier to understand, easier to follow, and easier to skim when trying to navigate lots of different moving pieces.

Step 3: Name & Claim The Whole Framework

You've slowed down and broken your larger insight into parts/steps…

You've Named & Claimed each meaningful milestone along the way…

Now, it's time to wrap the whole thing in a beautiful box.

Maybe something like **The 4-Step B2B Software Closer: 4 Simple Steps To Land Any Business Deal In Record Time.**

This way of breaking things down into steps and then reassembling them into a nice, neat box readers can carry around with them everywhere they go is how all legendary writers become known for certain ideas—regardless of whether or not those ideas are 100% original. Very often, it's the writer who differentiates herself or himself by Naming & Claiming the new way of thinking that becomes known for the idea. Case in point: *The 4-Hour Work Week* by Tim Ferriss, or *The Tipping Point* by Malcolm Gladwell. Both these books covered topics that many other people had written about (passive income & working smart not hard / word-of-mouth marketing). But these authors were the first ones to break them apart and then reassemble them using their own languaging—forever known for the thing they Named & Claimed as their own.

These timeless writing principles should be at the heart of your business newsletter.

Look closely, and we're doing the same thing here in this book you're reading right now (this is so meta). What is this? ***This is a framework for how you can create your own framework.*** *And all we're doing is slowing down, thinking about how we create our own frameworks (in steps), naming each step for you (so you can go through the steps too), and then calling it something: A Pirate's Framework For Creating Frameworks.*

How To Share New Insights

Finally, great writing doesn't just share new information.

Sometimes, great writing interprets old information in new ways.

If writing is thinking, then what readers are really paying for (with their attention or dollars or both) is *your* thinking—or, more specifically, **how your thinking changes their thinking.** Like buying the newest version of software, readers want your writing to upgrade the way they see the world. So, if you were to (literally) write out all the ways this "new upgrade" was going to improve their hardware (brain), what would you say? This is an exercise in brutal honesty, and always reveals where your writing/thinking is still undifferentiated (which is a good thing—now you know what to fix!).

Here are some ways to discover new insights to share:

- **Unlikely Intersections:** Anytime you can combine two or more topics, data points, or stories together, you can usually uncover something unique to share. To discover more and more "different" insights, combine more and more "different" categories. For example, what can the financial world learn from teenage gamers who win millions of dollars playing video games competitively? Or what can deforestation trends tell us about the future of real estate development? Smash two seemingly unrelated topics/categories together, and you'll stumble into a world of opportunity. Freakonomics is a great example of this: an economist's lens applied to the way society (not the economy) works. And if you really want to have some fun with this, remember: A Super of 1 category is a Super of 9 other categories.

- **Personal Stories:** Another way to present unique insights is to dig into your own personal experiences, "pull back the curtain," and let readers into your world and what it is you know—either through direct experience or by proximity to others who are educated on the subject. For example, one of Pirate Cole's most-read articles is a piece he wrote after writing for *Inc Magazine* for almost three years titled, *5 Myths I Learned About "Exposure" I Learned By Writing 400+ Columns For Inc Magazine*. The unique insight here comes from personal experience, and presents a POV only someone who has "lived it" can share.

- **Category Lens:** But our favorite way to present new insights to readers is to run whatever topic you are discussing through your own "category lens." One writer who does this fantastically well is Joe Pompliano (who, in record time, built an audience of more than 300,000 followers on Twitter and a newsletter list of nearly 50,000 subscribers). His category is Money & Sports (notice the unlikely intersection). With this category in mind, he then capitalizes on many trending topics and news stories by writing about the topic through his category lens. As long as he can bring things back to the unlikely intersection of Money & Sports, he continues to give readers the value he promised—and become more and more known for this niche he owns.

3. Write with courage.

> *"We're not concerned about the odds. And we're not concerned about winning or losing. We're here because it's the right place, the right thing to do, and the right time to do it."* —Russell Means (As told to Pirate Christopher by Founder of Sea Shepherd Captain Paul Watson)

If you wait to say what you know to be true, you are forgoing one of your greatest differentiation advantages.

This is what's known as Virtue Signaling—or, in the world of business, Virtue Marketing.

Virtue Marketing is where you say the same "new & different" thing as everyone else because now it's safe to do so. Remember at the beginning of COVID when every big company in the world created their own "we're going to get through this together" ad? They all sounded the same. Literally. Same music, same script, same message. When you do this, you are not speaking with courage. You are Virtue Marketing. You are standing up only because someone else stood up, and now it has been determined that it's safe to stand up.

Which makes you a coward.

Virtue Marketing was prevalent everywhere at the beginning of COVID (notice how, once the virtue has been sufficiently marketed, companies stop?), as it was when George Floyd was murdered in 2020 and protests filled the streets. Many companies waited to put out press releases to share how they felt about the situation (because they didn't know "what to say"). Then, a few weeks later, after a few courageous people spoke up and said what needed to be said, everyone else finally got around to publishing their own copy/pasted, "Our-hearts-go-out…" statements too. Because it was "safe" to do so.

Again, this is not what courageous people do.

Writing with courage means taking a stand for what you believe in *at a time when standing up means standing alone.*

Writing with courage means putting something at risk.

There can be no courage in the absence of danger.

The reason so many companies (and news outlets, publications, and individual journalists) go unheard is because the vast majority do everything they can to give the appearance of "saying something important" without putting themselves at risk. And that's why no one listens. Because in order to say something important and *different*, in order to write with courage, you have to put some chips on the table. You have to have something to lose.

No one wrote with more courage in the wake of George Floyd's murder than Dave Chapelle.

One of the most outlandish, over-the-top comedians of our generation, Dave Chappelle took a huge risk with his special titled *8:46* (the amount of time the police officer kneeled on

George Floyd's neck, ultimately killing him). The risk was: it wasn't a comedy special. It wasn't comedy at all. Do a quick Google search on the special and you'll find dozens of headlines like this one: "Netflix's new Dave Chapelle special '8:46' is no laughing matter." And according to NBC, "8:46 is successful because it is less of a standup routine and more a group therapy session for Black America." If you watched *8:46,* you probably spent more time questioning your own racial biases than you did laughing.

That was the risk Dave Chapelle took. And as a result, people listened.

Too often, writers, content creators, marketers, and even entrepreneurs and executives try to play a game called "standing out without standing up."

This is the aspiration of being seen as different without actually being different.

It's the desire to gain the outsized attention that can come from being different without suffering any of the criticism, backlash, or misunderstanding that happens along the way. But making a difference requires the courage to be different. And like many things today, people want the reward without the risk—the glory without traversing the territory.

> *This is the Jussie Smollett-ing of the world: being so thirsty for praise you are willing to stage your own attack to get it. The military has a term for this: Stolen Valor. And in a world of hacks, viral clickbait, and blitzscaling, an entire generation of creators have been lulled into playing*

> *this short-term game.*

For example, Cathie Wood (arguably one of the most influential, successful, and beloved hedge fund managers in the world today) says, in the early days of ARK, "So many people thought it was such an awful decision, and we had so much visibility, that when we started to gain traction, when the inflows started, it was like a headfake. And it got us so much more attention than we would have gotten otherwise." And so the real question is, in order to ultimately achieve outsized attention, are you willing to be seen as wrong until eventually the world realizes you were right?

Most people say "Yes" to this question.

But their actions say "NO WAY."

4. Don't be a curator of recycled stupidities.

The world doesn't need another marketing newsletter.

The world doesn't need another health & wellness website.

And the world doesn't need another business publication.

But what the world also doesn't need is you curating recycled stupidities—either someone else's or your own.

There's an amazing scene in the movie *The Big Short* where the stupidity of Collateralized Debt Obligations gets explained.

> *"You want me to really blow your mind? When the market deems a bond too risky to buy, what do you think we do with it? Take a guess. You think we just warehouse it on the books? No. We repackage it with a bunch of other shit that didn't sell and put it into a C.D.O."*

This is essentially how most companies treat their newsletters. They take a bunch of content nobody was reading from their company blog, package it into a "Weekly Digest," and hit publish. The result? The company might have 1,000,000 emails on their email list, but their open rate is 5%, 3%, sometimes less than 1%.

Again, the goal is not to have "a newsletter." The goal is to *share thinking that changes other people's thinking.*

The goal is to *make a difference*.

If you are a content curator, you better be a world-class curator.

There are only two ways to build an audience:

- Creating Content
- Curating Content

In the world of business media, most of the publications and newsletters at this point are content curators. These platforms realized that content creation is hard work, and it's a whole lot easier to just curate other people's content. Curation means sharing or summarizing someone else's ideas instead of coming up with your own.

Now, there's nothing wrong with being a content curator. In fact, there is tremendous potential in being a content curator in industries, verticals, and categories where finding a specific type of information is hard. (For example: there are hundreds of thousands of business podcasts. If you're interested in, say, cryptocurrencies, wouldn't you also be interested in subscribing to a weekly newsletter that summarized all the biggest takeaways, from all the biggest business podcasts who talked about crypto that week?) Additionally there are news and information outlets that curate content for specific audiences, saving people a ton of time Googling. These can be valuable sources.

The problem is when writers, content creators, and businesses think curating "anything" is going to be valuable to readers. Listen, just because you spent 20 minutes gathering three links doesn't mean your newsletter is valuable. And 100% of the time, readers can tell—you did your homework at the last minute.

If you are going to be a content curator, you need to a) be organizing the content you are curating within a new & different niche, and b) curate content from creators in a way that is MATERIALLY DIFFERENT from all the original content being created. When someone reads your work, it should feel like the equivalent of downloading 10x the information, from 10x more sources, in 10x less time.

5. Don't write inane garbage with the intention of "clickbaiting" people's attention.

This is an actual *Inc Magazine* article headline:

This Is What Jeff Bezos, Elon Musk, and 13 Other Successful Leaders Eat for Breakfast Every Day

Pirates, if we ever start writing things like this, please get us nice and drunk and then push us overboard (without a life jacket... ***Arrrrrrr!***).

Your goal—as a writer, creator, marketer, or business owner—is not to capture attention *for attention's sake*. Your newsletter should be as much of a treasure map for your readers and prospective customers as it is a treasure trove of data for you, your team, and your company. We love looking at the data for each and every Category Pirates newsletter we write & publish. We love seeing which topics prompt the most shares, spark the most discussion in the comments, and lead to the most questions. Because all this data tells us what YOU (fellow Pirate) find most interesting and valuable, and where we should spend more of our time, energy, and effort. (We are deeply inspired by Walt Disney's insight on this: "We don't make movies to make money, we make money to make more movies.")

But writing mindless "clickbaity" attention-grabbing garbage?

It's a waste of time for your readers, and tells you absolutely nothing about what else you should write in the future.

The more you write, the more you write.

Pirate Cole has a sea song he loves to sing and it goes like this: the more you write, the more data you gather, the more you learn what readers want and value, the more ideas you have, the more you write.

When you set out on the path of writing clickbait for the sake of attracting short-term attention, what you are really doing is building a hollow flywheel. (Not to mention turning yourself into an asshole.) You aren't actually learning anything about your readers. You aren't creating content that has the ability to compound on itself. You aren't building a library. You're just another hamster on the clickbait hamster wheel.

The best newsletters, publications, authors, and columnists don't do this. Instead, they take a long-term approach and focus on building a library of content with a common thread (a category), with a unique and different voice (AKA POV) so they can become known for a niche they own. Over time, that library grows, and grows, until it eventually becomes a rabbit hole new and curious readers get lost in with delight. Have you ever discovered a writer, read one of their posts and loved it, only to find out they have an archive with hundreds of other posts for you to explore? It's an exciting feeling. Finding that archive feels like discovering buried treasure.

If you want to start a newsletter (free or paid) and build a direct relationship with your audience, then give up the short-term game.

Don't chase virality. Chase LEGENDARY. Do the work you want to read. Create your favorite newsletter. Bet big on your different POV. (Even if you fail, wouldn't you rather go down fighting for something you think matters?) Most of all, don't get caught up trying to attract attention for attention's sake. Focus on your POV and getting to know your readers: Who are they? What do they value? What questions do they have? Why are they attracted to your different thinking?

Then set out to answer your readers' questions, in detail, day after day, week after week, month after month.

6. Don't confuse length with value.

When we first started Category Pirates, we saw advice everywhere on the Internet that said things like:

- "Don't start a newsletter. There are too many newsletters today and nobody is going to read yours."
- "People want 'value bombs.' They want short, bite-sized

content. Nobody is going to read 3,000+ words per newsletter. Keep them short. ~500 words."
- "Written content is dead. Nobody reads anymore. It's all videos now. You should start a TikTok page. Maybe incorporate some dancing. *People love dancing pirates! LOL!*"
- "People don't want to think. You can't give them anything too complicated. You have to dumb it down."

All sorts of stuff we didn't agree with (we don't believe our readers are 3rd graders looking to be told to *hustle, hustle, hustle!*).

And yet, the precise moment we decided to **double** the length of our weekly newsletters was when we saw our biggest spike in growth. So much so, we had to stop calling them "newsletters" and start calling them "mini-books" (languaging to reframe for our readers what they were receiving in their inboxes every week).

Now, don't get it confused: longer doesn't necessarily mean "more valuable." Writers and content creators make this mistake constantly, thinking if they just outsource the work to some cost-effective freelancer to "make it longer," readers will see it as "more valuable." But this usually ends up having the inverse effect—readers can tell.

Instead of chasing word count, we want to share with you an old saying in the sales copywriting world that goes like this: *"Who knows if your prospect will read 1,000 words or 3,000 words or 300 words of your sales letter; but if you write about them, and their problems, and how they can solve them, and their hopes and dreams, and how they can achieve them, they'll read 100,000 words and then ask for more."*

Once you know what it is readers want from you and what they value most, giving them *more* is never going to be a bad thing. Ever. No *Harry Potter* fan ever said, "No thanks J.K. Rowling, I've had enough of the story." When you love something, and when that *something* fills a void in your life—gives you a positive feeling, answers your questions, keeps you "in the know," or makes you feel understood—you will *never not* want more of it.

In a world of bite-sized content, depth can be a differentiator.

Instead of staying surface level, you can be the one who takes readers down to the depths.

You can be the one to put them in some scuba gear and help them explore the seafloor. (It's amazing what you find in places people rarely look.)

Especially when it comes to newsletters and long-form written content, if you are in the game of brevity, you probably have a differentiation problem. You don't actually know what your readers want—and so, as a result, you just spray & pray. You say, "Here check this out. And this. And this. And this. Have a great week!"

But the newsletters readers value most are the ones that *change their lives.* Think about that. Forget the fact that it's a "newsletter" for a second. What readers value is the *thinking,* and the degree to which the thinking *influences their own thinking.* And to be blunt, for the vast majority of topics, your thinking doesn't change very much after reading a 30-word tweet or a 250-word bite-sized newsletter. Thinking requires nuance, and nuance takes a bit of time to explain.

7. Reject the premise.

Finally, this is the most important point of all:

Legendary writing, *legendary thinking*, rejects the premise.

It doesn't "dive right in." Before the first word is spoken, legendary thinking asks the question, "Are we even asking the right question to begin with?"

For example: we started this chapter by saying how the three of us pirates came together to write a book on Category Design. Until, one day, we did some *thinking about thinking.* We asked ourselves, "Are we writing a book? Or are we writing dozens of mini-books?" By considering a different question (and reframing what we were doing), we had an *"Ah-ha! We're not just writing a book. We love working together and want to have a long-term relationship with each other and our readers about a topic we care deeply about."* Had we never asked this question, had we never stopped to *reject the premise*, we would have never started Category Pirates, the newsletter—which then allowed us to write multiple books at the same time.

Too often, writers and creators focus on *the writing*. They just want to get started. "We need to pump out 800 words, *every Tuesday*, for the rest of our lives, *so that we can start capturing emails and building an audience."* But this mentality tends to lead nowhere except a whole lot of busywork.

Instead, it's worth taking some *time* to reject the premise of your original thought. (Even if you come back to your original premise, rejecting it for a moment allows you to stress-test your thinking.) Should you even start a newsletter in the first place? What mission are you on? What sort of readers do you want to reach? Who do you want to help? And most importantly, in order to help those people, *what would be most valuable to them*? What kind of information? With what kind of voice? Presented in what form? A weekly newsletter? A series of videos? A podcast? Some combination of all the above?

Why 99% of newsletters fail:

If you want to know the real reason 99% of newsletters fail, and why the newsletter category as a whole is associated with terms of "inbox spam," it's because the vast majority of people who start newsletters *just want to start a newsletter.* It's a means to an end. They want to "attract attention," they want to "build an audience," they want to "gather leads," they want to "make money." But notice, all of these things benefit the creator, not the reader. They are selfish wants. More importantly, they are outcomes. They are things you experience as a byproduct of successfully helping other people, educating them, entertaining them, and changing their thinking in a positive, valuable way.

So, our advice to you is this:

If you want to write a top 1% business newsletter, don't set out to write a top 1% business newsletter.

If you want to create content that goes viral, don't worry about going viral.

If you want your marketing campaigns to be written about in all the major publications for how "creative" they are, don't deploy marketing campaigns with the North Star goal of being written about in all the major publications for how "creative" they are.

Instead, set out on a mission to help someone—one very specific type of person.

Learn everything you can about their wants, needs, fears, and desires. Talk to them. Ask them questions. Make lists of everything they need to know in order to be successful. Present them with solutions and then ask again, "Is this helpful? Do you need me to go into more depth?" Like we said, whether you present this information in a newsletter, a blog post, a podcast, a text message, or scroll delivered via carrier pigeon is irrelevant. If you can successfully solve people's problems by providing them with insights, frameworks, stories, and new perspectives, they will go to great lengths to receive that information from you.

Conversely, it doesn't matter how convenient you make the content: if the reader doesn't value what you're saying, they won't give you their attention.

Subscribe To Category Pirates

ARRRRRRRRR, fellow Pirates!
  Did you enjoy this book on category design?

We would love for you to hop aboard the pirate ship and join us.

Categorypirates.substack.com

Each week, we publish a "mini-book" (5,000 to 10,000+ words) on the topic of category design and send it straight to your inbox (similar to the chapters of this book). And while we republish our "mini-books" on other platforms (like Amazon), the Category Pirates paid newsletter is our primary destination. There, our "mini-books" are more interactive, and we are better able to connect with readers like you directly.

In addition, you receive access to our entire archive of "mini-books," full of timeless frameworks, stories, and case studies on how to design & dominate new categories in the world.

We hope to see you aboard the pirate ship!

Made in United States
Orlando, FL
12 April 2023